PERCY BYSSHE SHELLEY
POET AND PIONEER

BY

HENRY S. SALT,

KENNIKAT PRESS, INC./PORT WASHINGTON, N. Y.

PERCY BYSSHE SHELLEY

First Published in 1896
Reissued in 1968 by Kennikat Press
Library of Congress Catalog Card No: 68-16285
Manufactured in the United States of America

CONTENTS

Tu, pater, es rerum inventor, tu patria nobis
Suppeditas præcepta, tuisque ex, inclute, chartis,
Floriferis ut apes in saltibus omnia libant,
Omnia nos itidem depascimur aurea dicta,
Aurea, perpetua semper dignissima vita.

Thou art the father of our faith, and thine
Our holiest precepts ; from thy songs divine,
As bees sip honey in some flowery dell,
Cull we the glories of each golden line,
Golden, and graced with life imperishable.

LUCRETIUS.

PREFACE

THE aim of this book, which is now re-issued in what seems likely to be its final form, is not to tell anew that story of Shelley's life which has been fully told by Dr. Dowden and other biographers; nor to throw light on doubtful passages in the text, as has been amply done by Mr. H. Buxton Forman; but rather to make clear, as the most conclusive answer to much that has been written about Shelley's "vagueness," the very direct and important relation in which he stands towards certain great modern movements.

"Shall we ever know the truth about Shelley in any particular?" was the despairing cry of a rather uncongenial student of the poet.[1] Perhaps not; but it should be our desire to know the truth about him, not so much in any "particular" as in the main features of his character and in the governing purpose of his life. "The rule of criticism," as Shelley himself remarked, "to be adopted in judging of the life, actions, and words of a man who has acted any

---

[1] Mr. Andrew Lang, *Fortnightly Review*, February, 1907.

conspicuous part in the revolutions of the world, ought not to be narrow. We ought to form a general image of his character and doctrines, and refer to this whole the distinct portions of action and speech by which they are diversified."

Only by keeping this principle in view is it possible to frame a clear picture of Shelley from the conflicting and often untrustworthy stories of his early biographers; for it must frankly be said that no positive belief can be placed in any unsupported assertion made by Hogg, Peacock, or Trelawny. Lies of the first magnitude stare us in the face in Hogg's so-called *Life*. Peacock's incapacity for understanding Shelley may be judged from his cynical remark that, if the poet had lived to be seventy years old, he would have summed up his own record in the word "désillusionné." Trelawny was far more discerning; but only a very unsuspecting reader would take quite literally the reminiscences of that picturesque "pirate's" old age. No; the truth about Shelley can be gathered only from a careful sifting of the material which we possess, and from a free use of the interpreter's own judgment in accepting some statements and rejecting others.

I say "interpreter," not "critic," because, in view of the disastrous failure of criticism in its dealings with Shelley, we seem to need a new method and a new name. Sympathy alone can make his writings intelligible to us.   It is in the singular unity of Shelley's nature, in the consistency that throughout ruled his thought and actions, that we find the key to a right understanding of his genius.

H. S. S.

CHAPTER I.

RIVAL VIEWS OF SHELLEY

IT is very instructive to note the series of changes which public opinion has undergone, and is undergoing, with regard to Shelley's character. During the poet's life, and for some time after, his detractors had the field almost entirely to themselves, the voices raised on his behalf being those of a few personal friends or literary admirers who could scarcely make themselves heard amid the general chorus of detestation.[1] It is only by a study of the contemporary criticism of Shelley's poems that we can realise the intensity of the feeling aroused by his attack on the established religion and ethics, which seems to have filled his readers with a conviction that he was a monster of abnormal and almost superhuman wickedness.

> We feel [wrote one of these outraged moralists, in reference to *Queen Mab*[2]] as if one of the darkest of the fiends had been clothed with a human body to enable him to gratify his enmity against the human race, and as if the supernatural atrocity of his hate were only heightened by his power to do injury. So strongly has this impression dwelt upon our minds that we absolutely asked a friend who had seen this individual to describe him to us—as if a cloven foot, or horn, or flames from the mouth, must have marked the external appearance of so bitter an enemy to mankind.

In the same article Shelley is variously alluded to as

---

[1] Leigh Hunt in particular deserves grateful mention for his early recognition of Shelley.
[2] *Literary Gazette*, May 19, 1821.

"the fiend-writer," "the blaster of his race," and "the demoniac proscriber of his species." The Englishman who, meeting the poet in an Italian post-office, asked whether he was "that damned atheist, Shelley," and un-ceremoniously knocked him down, was merely translating into action the almost unanimous sentiment of his fellow-countrymen concerning the author of *Queen Mab*.

But as time went on, bringing with it a period of reform instead of repression, and as the disinterested nobleness of Shelley's character was vindicated in the narratives of Hogg, Medwin, and other biographers, while the high value of his poetry was recognised— slowly and reluctantly at first—by the more discerning critics, it gradually came about that he was viewed in a milder light by the succeeding generation of readers. A kindly though somewhat sorrowful tone was now adopted towards him, a real admiration for his poetical genius and personal sincerity being tempered by a stern censure, more in grief than anger, of the misguided principles on which his life was framed.

Thus he no longer figured as a deliberate scoundrel, fired with infernal animosity against the salvation of mankind, but as a wild enthusiast, possessed of many noble instincts, though unhappily warped and perverted by the sophisms of Godwin and other mischievous innovators. Had religion been differently represented to him; had he been more wisely educated by those who had charge of him in his youth; had he studied history more carefully, or conversed with Coleridge, or enjoyed some other advantage which his fate withheld— then, it was argued, Shelley's career would have been a wholly different one, and, to quote the words of Gilfillan, we should have seen the demoniac "clothed, and in his right mind, sitting at the feet of Jesus."

"Poor, poor Shelley," exclaimed Frederick Robertson, when he meditated on these touching possibilities; and his words give us the keynote of this particular phase of Shelley criticism. The age of abuse and vilification had now become obsolete, and the "poor, poor Shelley" era had succeeded it.

This, it is important to note, has been the prevailing conception of Shelley's character for the last fifty years, though there have not been wanting signs that it is destined to be replaced in its turn by a new and more accurate interpretation. For in spite of occasional outbursts which may be regarded as a survival or recrudescence of the abusive period—belated bottles of a sour old vintage, which explode from time to time in the changed atmosphere of a later day—the main tendency of the age has been distinctly towards a more genial estimate of Shelley, a view which has been fully, and perhaps finally, expressed in the work of Dr. Edward Dowden, whose opinion of Shelley's ethics may be summed up in the judgment he pronounces on *Queen Mab*, that "such precipitancy may constitute a grave offence against social morality, yet we may dare to love the offender."

But the apologetic view of Shelley, which asks that the poet's social heresies may be forgiven him in consideration of the beauty of his poems and the devoted though mistaken earnestness of his life, will be found to be an untenable one, however gracious and welcome it may be when contrasted with the old contumely of seventy years back; for it rests on the assumption that ennobling poetry can result from an immoral and therefore pernicious ideal. In estimating the lifework of such a character as Shelley's, it must surely be an error to set aside as valueless the central underlying convictions, while professing admiration for the poetry which resulted therefrom, as if the proverb "By their fruits ye shall know them" did not hold good in literature as elsewhere.

It will be shown in this volume that there can be no mistake whatever about the attitude which Shelley took up, not in *Queen Mab* only, but in the whole body of his writings, towards the established system of society, which, as he avowed in one of his later letters, he wished to see "overthrown from the foundations, with all its superstructure of maxims and forms." His principles are utterly subversive of all that orthodoxy holds most sacred, whether in ethics or in religion : if he was wrong in them, he is deserving of the severest possible blame ; if right, of equally unstinted praise. In neither event is there any ground for the apologetic theory, which, by its vague and vacillating attempt to reconcile the irreconcilable, has made an enigma out of a personality which is singularly intelligible and clear.

Now this denudation of Shelley, by readers who could appreciate what is called the "pure poetry" of the *Sensitive Plant* or the *Cloud*, but were horrified at the anarchic doctrines of *Queen Mab* or *Laon and Cythna*, has been a remarkable and instructive process. The poet who, above all others, has been a source of strength and inspiration to social and ethical reformers, whose lines were familiar watchwords in great democratic movements such as Chartism and Freethought; this great revolutionary poet has been reduced by our dilettante men of letters to a mere singer and sentimentalist [1]—has been compassionated, and patronised, and white-washed, and apologised for, and forgiven, until we have before us

---

[1] As, for instance, in Mr. Edmund Gosse's reference, in his address at the Shelley centenary celebration, to the poet's "shining garments, so little specked with mire." See, too, the essay on Shelley by Francis Thompson, written from the Catholic standpoint.

a meaningless and impossible nondescript, a monster, half idiot, half angel, who is alleged to have built up a noble personality, and an immortal fabric of song, on a foundation of thought which the critics, in so far as they have condescended to examine it at all, have pronounced, with almost one accord, to be visionary, rotten, or immoral.

Against this, the orthodox and sentimental view of Shelley, there remains now to be set the rational and scientific one, the view which has all along been held by a handful of sympathisers, but has only begun within recent years to attract any considerable share of attention. According to this newer estimate, Shelley was the poet-pioneer of the great democratic movement; he anticipated, in his own character and aspirations, many of the revolutionary ideas now in process of development. We do not assert that he was a faultless being, that he was free from eccentricities and foibles, or that he did not share some of the intellectual errors of his time; but we do say that his outlook, far from being that of a weak-minded visionary, was, in the main, an exceptionally shrewd one, inasmuch as all the chief principles which were essential to his creed are found to have increased enormously in importance during the years that have passed since his death.

We hold that this philosophy of Shelley's must be considered together with, and not apart from, his poetry, that the two are inextricably connected and interwoven, and that Shelley the poet is to a large extent unintelligible, when dissociated, as he is still commonly dissociated, from Shelley the pioneer. The central facts of his life, and the leading points of his life-creed, are obvious and unmistakable. He may have been the " fiend-writer " that his early critics represented him ; he certainly was not the nincompoop of Matthew Arnold's epigram, the "beautiful and ineffectual angel, beating in the void his luminous wings in vain." Imbecility is never beautiful ; and an angel, however luminous, who should conduct himself in such manner, would be a far less ornamental personage than the sootiest denizen of the pit.

Indeed, in thus shutting their eyes to the ideas that inspired Shelley's writings, while sentimentalising about the purity of his character and the ethereal beauty of his song, modern critics have invented an even more monstrous personage than the sulphureous Shelley of their forefathers, that demon with whom it was at least possible to transact business on the basis of his demonhood. It was at any rate an intelligible conception of Shelley, in an age when to be a revolutionist was regarded as synonymous with being a scoundrel ; and for this reason I am now inclined to think that Mr. Cordy Jeaffreson's view of the poet, as set forth in *The Real Shelley*, was a work of greater insight than most of us were at first ready to allow. We were prejudiced against the book by the rancorous tone which makes itself so unpleasantly evident on a number of minor matters ; and we thus overlooked or underestimated its one great merit. Mr. Jeaffreson at least saw, though from a hostile standpoint, the *importance* of Shelley's opinions. His book was a forlorn hope, a last attempt to stem the rising tide of appreciation, and to show that the earlier and satanical Shelley was in very truth the "real" one. Such an attempt was necessarily doomed to be a failure ; but it may be that this recognition, however offensively expressed, was a greater compliment to Shelley than the vapid praises of the apologists. It is " better to reign in Hell than serve in Heaven "; better to be an effectual demon, with that "power to do injury" of which the early critic complained, than an "ineffectual angel" patronised by literary prigs.

For why is it that many distinguished and learned men who have undertaken to enlighten the world concerning Shelley have failed so grotesquely that even the efforts of the Quarterly Reviewers seem successful by comparison? Simply because, with every intention to be just, they were devoid of that insight into the objects of Shelley's gospel which is essential to a right understanding of his life. Wanting this, they have seen only chaos and indecision in a career which was remarkable for its directness of aim, and have heard only what Carlyle described as "inarticulate wail" in the clearest trumpet-call that ever poet sounded; and having thus created, out of the dust of their own minds, a mythical personage still more unreal than the "Real Shelley" of Mr. Cordy Jeaffreson, they have proceeded to express their virtuous astonishment at the perplexing and contradictory nature of this phantom of their own imagining.

Mr. Walter Bagehot, for example, was so amazed at the perversities of Shelley's intellect, as viewed from the Bagehottian standpoint, that he set him down as actuated by mere impulse rather than by a reasoning faculty.

Mr. Leslie Stephen, too, having no sympathy with revolutionary ideas, would not allow Shelley credit for even average powers of thought, but asserted that "that which is really admirable is not the vision itself, but the pathetic sentiment caused by Shelley's faint recognition of its obstinate insubstantiality."

Even Mr. J. A. Symonds, whose pleasant monograph is valued by all Shelley students, was misled by the same prejudice when he stated that "the blending in him of a pure and earnest purpose with moral and social theories

that could not but have proved pernicious to mankind at
large, produced at times an almost grotesque mixture in
his actions no less than in his verse." But how if these
theories should *not* prove so pernicious as Mr. Symonds
assumed them to be? And in that case what becomes
of the "grotesque mixture" in Shelley's actions and
character?[1]

The fact is, that the majority of critics, while doing
honour to Shelley's poetical genius and exalted enthusiasm, have altogether underrated the keenness of his
insight into the problems of modern times. Being accus-
tomed, by the force of class tradition, to ignore the
Shelleyan ideals—that is, the fountain-head of the poet's
singing—they have inevitably failed to enter into the
spirit of his song. His book of prophecy lies open before
them, but must remain in great part unintelligible, until
sympathy, the sole clue to the understanding of a new
gospel, shall put an end to the foolish talk about the
"incoherence" of Shelley's message and the "hallucinations" of his brain.[2]

Without at all forgetting the great literary services that
have been rendered to Shelley's writings during the past
quarter-century, I deny that he can be fully understood,
even as a poet, under the present form of society, unless
by those, and scarcely even by those, who look for the
changes which he looked for, and desire to hasten that
bloodless revolution which was at once the theme and the
inspiration of his song. As the number of such reformers
increases (and it is increasing very sensibly at the present

[1] In a letter dated July 1, 1892, Mr. Symonds wrote to me as follows:
" Since I wrote the little book to which you allude, I have changed some of
my views in your direction."
[2] See the fine sonnet on Shelley in Thomas Wade's *Poems and Sonnets*
(1835), concluding thus :—

Men profane,
Blaspheme thee : I have heard thee dreamer styled.
I've mused upon their wakefulness, and smiled.

time), the apologetic view of Shelley will gradually pass away, and in its place we shall have the appreciative view, which will honour England's greatest lyric poet, not on the absurd ground that he sang beautifully and pathetically on behalf of a foolish and wicked cause, but because, seeing clearly that the current forms of religion and morals would have to be revolutionised, he expressed that conviction, which each succeeding year is proving to be a true conviction, in words of consummate tenderness and power.

This new method of Shelley criticism is not merely in prospect, but has already commenced. It was heralded by James Thomson's remarkable article contributed to the *National Reformer* as long ago as 1860, and by the memoir which Mr. W. M. Rossetti prefixed to his edition of the poems ten years later—a strong and sensible piece of writing, which was, as far as I know, the first consider-able contribution to Shelleyan literature in which, not the poetry only, but the conceptions that determined the poetry, were treated with due seriousness, and without a word of that unhappy extenuation or patronage which strikes so false a note in many other essays. As to the valuable critical work done by Mr. Rossetti, Mr. Buxton Forman, Dr. Garnett, Dr. Dowden, and others, it may truly be said to have been instrumental in preparing the way for a better understanding of Shelley in his ethical as well as his literary character.

We see, therefore, that the angelic Shelley is moribund, that he is beginning to go the way of his satanic prede-cessor, and that he will not long continue to beat his luminous wings in vain, either in the void or elsewhere. If Shelley was what he is commonly represented to have been, an amiable enthusiast and visionary; and if, as Mr. Leslie Stephen assured us, "the crude incoherence

of his whole system is too obvious to require exposition,"
we might reasonably have expected that the years which
have passed since the death of this deluded dreamer
would have scattered his hallucinations to the winds.
Yet, strange to say, Mr. Leslie Stephen himself complained, and in the same essay, that "the devotees of
some of Shelley's pet theories have become much noisier
than they were when the excellent Godwin ruled his little
clique." But is it not, on the face of it, a rather remarkable fact that a system so crude as to need no refutation
should be thus steadily gaining new adherents after more
than three-quarters of a century? The inference seems
to be that Shelley's vision was a good deal more pene-
trating than that of some of his critics.

Do we claim, then, it is sometimes asked, that Shelley
was an "original" thinker? Perhaps not—in that sense
which implies the contribution of brand-new ideas to
philosophy or ethics. Shelley's social views, as every-
one knows, were largely drawn from Rousseau and the
French school, from Thomas Paine, William Godwin, and
Mary Wollstonecraft; but, while borrowing freely, he
could also freely assimilate and vitalise. There is an
originality in the selection and treatment, as well as in
the promulgation, of ideas; and this faculty, this "reasoning instinct all divine," Shelley possessed in an eminent
degree. He grasped and assimilated those democratic
ideals which were destined to survive; and if his creed
be compared with that of the other poets and thinkers of
his age, in the light of the history of the past century, it
is not Shelley who will be found deficient in sagacity and
foresight.

But though thus inspired, Shelley was by nature and
temperament essentially a poet. He was the poet-
prophet of the great humanitarian revival; and as he

sang of the future rather than of the present, and of a distant future rather than of a near one, there is of necessity a vagueness in many of his poetical utterances, though this is fortunately to a great extent corrected and counterbalanced by the clearness of his prose essays. An attempt is sometimes made to discount the effect of his writings on the score of his youthfulness; he had not time, it is said, to mature his own thoughts, much less to instruct those of other people. This objection, however, can hardly be taken very seriously; for, in the first place, opinions must stand or fall by their intrinsic worth, and not by the age of their advocate; and secondly, as Shelley himself said to Trelawny, "the mind of man, his brain, and nerves, are a truer index of his age than the calendar."

The object of this book is not to attribute to Shelley an impossible perfection, but to point out that he was a pioneer of a movement which, whether for good or evil, is steadily advancing in interest and importance. The recognition of Shelley the man is beginning to follow hard on that of Shelley the poet; and though there is little doubt that those critics who, like the late Mr. H. D. Traill, deprecate anything more than "the very baldest and briefest statement of the facts of the poet's life," are truly expressing the disinclination of the privileged classes to hear more than they are obliged to hear of this most persistent prophet of reform, yet it must be already apparent that this naive injunction of silence will produce exactly as much impression on the study of Shelley as did Canute's imperial prohibition on the flowing tide.

CHAPTER II.

HEIR TO FIELD PLACE

A GREAT revolutionary outbreak is something more than a sundering of the bondages of the past; it is a rent, however momentary, in the veil that divides us from the future. Through that rent, as by a lightning-flash, the near is fused in the remote, and men have glimpses, though but broken and partial glimpses, of far regions which later centuries shall inherit. Future ideas, future hopes, future faiths, and future freedom—these, and a thousand germs of realities not yet realised, are poured into the lap of the present, there to grow and fructify when the moment that gave them birth is forgotten. Is it possible, at such great crises, that the heart and soul of man, *as he will be*, are in some rare instances anticipated and incarnated in the form of man *as he is* ?

Shelley has often been called the child of the French Revolution. It is my purpose to depict him, not according to the common notion, as merely an impassioned singer and wild-hearted visionary, full of noble though misdirected enthusiasm, and giving promise of better things if his brief life had been prolonged, but rather as one who was charged with a sacred mission, which was seriously undertaken and faithfully fulfilled. His life and writings were a mirror held up to our present social system from without ; he came like a messenger from another planet to denounce and expose the anomalies that exist on the earth, to show the glaring contrast between might and right, law and justice, ephemeral custom and essential piety.[1]

It has sometimes been the humour of imaginative minds to illustrate this contrast between the conventional and the natural by the story of a supposed visit to a fabled " Utopia " or " New Atlantis "; or the process has been reversed, and the follies and frailties of artificial society have been shown through the medium of some " Chinese philosopher " or intelligent " Traveller from New Zealand "; or, yet again, as in William Morris's *News from Nowhere,* the writer has projected himself in a dream into the happier commonweal of the future, and has thus emphasised the evils and miseries of the present. But Shelley largely embodied in his own person and feelings what other writers have but fancifully suggested, and the moral at which they have hinted was by him directly enforced. He was *himself* the visitor from another region, and the Utopia from which he came was indeed nothing else than a future phase of society. He anticipated a later period of social and moral evolution; his gospel of humanity was the creed of a new era that is slowly dawning on mankind.

A life devoted to such a message involves, in the very nature of things, a subjection to misunderstanding and abuse from the majority of one's fellow-mortals. The man who is born a few centuries before his kindred age must be, in relation to contemporary thought and institutions, a man devoid of piety and reverence : he stands towards public opinion somewhat as a cultured and liberal thinker of to-day would stand towards the customs and prejudices of the middle ages, could such a

[1] " He was like a spirit that had darted out of its orb and found itself in another world. I used to tell him that he had come from the planet Mercury " (Leigh Hunt).

one be suddenly plunged back into the society of a past period, and invited to applaud the morality of the torture-chamber and the stake. It is for this reason that the pioneers of all great movements bring not peace into the world, but a sword; they are the disguised emissaries of the implacable Future, sent to sow dissension and heart-searching in the Present's comfortable camp.

And in Shelley's case, as though the anachronism of his birth were not sufficiently remarkable, all the attendant circumstances combined to intensify and accentuate it. That he should have been born heir to the typical country seat of a typical country family, and plunged into scenes and society from which his nature was utterly alien and remote, was surely the strangest defiance of all hereditary laws—an incongruity of fate for which not only the poet himself was to be compassionated, but, most of all, those deluded relatives who laid claim on him as kith and kin.

On August 4, 1792, there was probably no country gentleman in England who was better satisfied with himself, his position, and his prospects than Mr. Timothy Shelley, of Field Place, Horsham, Sussex. For on that day the felicity of his marriage with the beautiful Elizabeth Pilfold was crowned by the birth of a son, who was to all appearances destined to maintain the time-honoured traditions of the family. The heir to a wealthy estate, the child of a father who studied the interests of the Whig party in politics and the precepts of the accomplished Chesterfield in private life, he could scarcely fail to follow dutifully in the course which Providence had marked out for him. It could not be doubted that if he lived to manhood he would be a sturdy country squire of the old-fashioned sort, fond of his bottle of wine, devoted to field sports, and above all a determined upholder of orthodox and constitutional principles. Mr. Timothy Shelley, well-meaning and kind-hearted man that he was, felt that he could be the best of fathers to a son who promised to be so close a likeness of himself.

But as years passed on, and the child grew into a tall, slim boy, with great dreamy eyes, and long curling hair, his parents found themselves less and less able to forecast with confidence the future bent of his character. There was something strange and unaccountable about his manner and occupations which was out of harmony with the course of life at Field Place, and made him a puzzle and enigma to his anxious and disappointed relatives. It was naturally disquieting to a country gentleman's mind to hear that his son and heir, instead of employing his holidays in learning the ancestral art of killing pheasants and partridges, was in the habit of playing familiarly with a large snake on the lawn, or entertaining his infant sisters with stories of an aged alchemist, said to have his abode in certain disused garrets and passages of Field Place, or, worse still, endangering his own safety and that of the household by the recklessness of his chemical experiments. It was an unhealthy sign, too, that an English boy should care less for the society of grooms and gamekeepers than for solitary rambles about the Sussex lanes, and mysterious nocturnal wanderings in which neither sense nor purpose could be discovered.

Then, again, the reports from Dr. Greenlaw, of whose school at Brentford he had now become an inmate, were far from encouraging. If Tom Medwin, his cousin and school-fellow, could get on well with masters and boys, why could not Bysshe do the same, since he might be presumed to be Tom's equal in ability? It was

doubtless provoking to the father to learn that his son
was ridiculed and teased by his school-fellows; and,
being a man of the world, he knew well that in such
cases it is the victim himself who is to blame; nor was
he any better pleased by a letter which Mrs. Shelley
received from Bysshe, giving a long account of a sentimental attachment to one of his school-fellows, whose
admirable qualities were described with much emphasis
and exaggeration.   Mrs. Shelley wisely decided to return
no answer to this letter, in the hope that her silence
might be a reproof to his emotional tendency, which was
probably fostered by the boy's unfortunate habit of
reading volume after volume of romance.

But of all Bysshe's singularities the most alarming to
his parents was his recital of imaginary scenes and conversations; for they clearly saw that this confusion of
the boundary-line between fact and fiction was a symptom
of an intellectual and moral laxity especially deplorable
in a boy of Bysshe's position.   Such eccentricities might
be smiled at or pardoned in the case of a poor aspirant
in art or literature; but they could not be tolerated in
one who was eventually to be a county magnate and
Whig member for the borough of Shoreham.

What did it all portend—snakes, alchemist, inflam-
mable liquids, star-gazings, and romance readings?   These
things were little to the liking of a sober-minded
country gentleman, who being by nature somewhat
irascible, would doubtless speak out rather strongly on
the subject of Bysshe's misdemeanours.   On the other
hand, there were occasions when Mr. Shelley was
inclined to feel proud of his son, and to become reconciled to the idea that he was going to be " clever " like
his grandfather, that rather eccentric old gentleman, who
at that very time was about to receive a baronetcy from

his leader, the Duke of Norfolk, in return for his past services to the Whig cause. Could it be that the boy was likely to prove what is called a genius? We are not told whether Mr. Shelley ever speculated on this point; but we may be quite sure that, if he did so, he looked forward with some complacency to the enlistment of Bysshe's powers on the side of social order, already threatened by the insidious doctrines of the revolutionary school. Whigs and Tories were at least agreed upon one point—that the strongholds of constitutionalism and religion must be henceforth defended with no uncertain hand against the enemy's increasing assaults.

It was a time when revolution was "in the air." The example of France and America had already given the signal for other national uprisings; Ireland was in a state of chronic commotion and overt rebellion; while in England certain mischievous agitators were busily engaged in "setting class against class," and were striving to impress the labourers and artisans with the wild notion that they were the victims of social injustice and oppression. One William Godwin had lately published a book named *Political Justice*, which Mr. Shelley doubtless heard spoken of as harmful and seditious; and it was possibly reported at Field Place, as an instance of the extreme depravity of the times, that a woman of the name of Wollstonecraft had been wicked enough to write a vindication of the supposed "rights" of her sex. The good old cause of the throne and the constitution was evidently in need of a champion; and if Bysshe, who seemed to be so unlike boys of his own age, should turn out to have talent, here was a worthy object for a youthful patriot's ambition.

Such, we may not unreasonably surmise, were the

expectations which the interloper known as Percy
Bysshe Shelley was destined in a brief course to shatter.
I shall not waste any labour on a task, to which some
Shelley critics have devoted time and temper, of estimating the rights and wrongs, the palliations and the
aggravations, of the antagonism between Shelley and
his father, which showed itself at an early date and
widened, as the years went on, into an open estrangement. No verdict of "bad son" or "bad father" is to
be given in such a case; the pathos of the position—a
typical position—lies far deeper than that. Estrangement, whether veiled or recognised, must inevitably
result between those who, albeit blood-relations, are by
temperament strangers from the first; and it is worse
than useless to allot praise or blame where there is no
single feeling in common. On the one side is the
Family, with its constant demand that each and all of
its members shall think and live in subjection to the
domestic ideal; on the other side is the young and
ardent spirit, possessed of larger aspirations and wider
aims, which realises that the true piety of life consists
neither in gratifying nor in mortifying self, but in faithfully following the highest line of self-development.
What compromise can there be between two such
adverse principles as these, when, as in Shelley's case,
neither the one nor the other can give way?

No complaint can be made against Shelley's father,
except that he was a country gentleman. There is no
adequate explanation of Shelley's revolt from his father,
except that he was not a country gentleman. Incidental
faults there doubtless were, on one side and the other;
but we need not be concerned to justify or apologise for
them. At the root of the whole matter lay the simple
fact that Shelley had no conception of "filial duty"; he

was in the ordinary parlance, and according to ordinary notions, an "unnatural son." That is to say, he could make no pretence of loving or reverencing his father because he was his father, or of consulting the interests of the Shelley family because his own name was Shelley. Throughout life he loved those whom he felt to be lovable, and he recognised no narrower family interests than the welfare of his fellow men.

The fetish of the family was the first idol against which Shelley rebelled, and by that rebellion betrayed at the very outset that he was indeed no native English growth, but a stranger from a far land. It was no fault of his that, heralding an age which shall have cast off the domestic ideal, he was prematurely launched into an age when that superstition was rife, and thereby involved in sorest trials and misunderstandings—sorer even than those by which sensitive childhood is not unfrequently perplexed. It was not his fault, but his misfortune, or rather it was a dramatically poignant condition of a rare and subtle destiny, that the most ethereal genius of English literature should have been born the heir to Field Place.

CHAPTER III.

THE EDUCATION OF A GENTLEMAN

MR. TIMOTHY SHELLEY now looked forward to his clever
son winning academical distinction, and thereafter filling
his place in Parliament with honour and success ; to gain
which end he was of opinion that he must give him the
advantage of the best education which an English youth
can enjoy. Himself a disciple of Chesterfield, he knew
the paramount importance of an easy grace of manner ;
he therefore determined to send the boy to Eton and
Oxford, where, in the contact with others of his own
social position, he would doubtless lose the eccentricities
by which his character was deformed. So this strange
scion of the Future, who, being ignorant of his own
origin, was not able to explain or protest, found himself
subjected, from the age of twelve years to eighteen, to no
less painful an ordeal than the education of a gentleman.
Let us take a brief view of him, as he underwent this
process, at each of the two venerable " seats of learning "
to which he was attached.[1]

A visitor to Eton College might have chanced to be a
witness of a " Shelley-bait," a strange and suggestive
spectacle, illustrative in a remarkable degree of the
temper and manners of the average English schoolboy

[1] "Yes, it is a seat of learning; it is a seat in which learning sits very
comfortably, well thrown back, as in an easy chair, and sleeps so soundly
that neither you nor I, nor anybody else, can wake her."—*Hogg's " Shelley
at Oxford."*

20

in his gregarious condition. A crowd of lads of various
sorts and sizes might have been seen encircling, jeering,
and persecuting a solitary boy, whose appearance differed
in some essential points of character from that of the
mass of his school-fellows. He was slight and graceful
in stature, and in the expression of his face there was
something wild and spiritual, yet at the same time full of
" exceeding sweetness and sincerity"; the other features
that arrested attention were the long dark brown hair
and the large, blue, earnest-looking eyes. In spite of his
brief paroxysms of rage, caused by the attacks of his
tormentors, he did not look like one who had been guilty
of any very heinous offence. What, then, was the crime
for which he had been outlawed from the good-will of his
fellows ?

It was a serious one; it was none other than the
unpardonable sin of rebelling against that great deity of
boys and men—Custom. This youthful iconoclast, who
answered to the name of Percy Bysshe Shelley, had
already commenced, to his infinite discredit and discomfort, to hold and advance certain opinions of his
own, which by no means coincided with the established
Etonian creed, the full acceptance of which was an
indispensable condition of school-boy salvation. A
decree, therefore, had gone forth that the criminal
should be known by the name of " Mad Shelley" and
"The Atheist," and should undergo a course of that
wholesome treatment which the faithful have so often
found effective for those who wander from the fold.
Who shall blame the Eton boys for acting as they did ?
A public school in such matters is but a microcosm—a
reflection of the greater world that lies around it and
beyond; and when a herd of schoolboys think fit to
tease and slander one who differs from his fellows, their

conduct is but typical of that of the over-grown school-boys of mature life.

But at any rate, it may be thought, the boy might have turned for consolation and protection to the masters who had undertaken the duty of educating him. Unfortunately there was little or no sympathy with Shelley in that quarter. Why should busy men take any special interest in an apparently half-crazy boy, whose Latin verses, although fluently written, were often lacking in metrical correctness, and who, instead of seeking distinction in the ordinary channels, persisted in following a line of study of his own, such as translating Pliny's *Natural History* and reading Godwin's *Political Justice*? To burn down willow-stumps with gunpowder, to keep an electric battery in one's room, and to send up fire-balloons by night, are doings not exactly calculated to win the approbation of a schoolmaster; and it is no wonder that Shelley's tutors, in their dislike of the eccentricities that lay on the surface of his nature, should have failed to discover the real underlying wealth.

So the poor outlaw, whose heart even now was full of love for every living being, and whose mind was aglow with the divine thirst for knowledge, could find no favour with either masters or boys, but pined in vain for the seclusion of his green Sussex lanes and the more congenial society of the friendly snake that haunted the lawn of Field Place. Sadly and slowly it dawned upon his mind that this life, which had seemed at first to be all fresh and pure and fair, was blighted by a withering curse —the curse of the tyranny which selfish and sordid natures inflict on the gentle and harmless.

It was in this mood and under these influences that Shelley, as he stood alone one May morning on the "glittering grass" of the Eton Playing Fields, was

visited by one of those sudden impulses by which many a
heroic spirit has been summoned, in a moment's inspiration, to take his part once and forever in the battle of life.

> I do remember well the hour which burst
> My spirit's sleep : a fresh May dawn it was,
> When I walked forth upon the glittering grass,
> And wept, I knew not why ; until there rose
> From the near schoolroom, voices that, alas !
> Were but one echo from a world of woes—
> The harsh and grating strife of tyrants and of foes.
>
> And then I clasped my hands and looked around—
> But none was near to mock my streaming eyes,
> Which poured their warm drops on the sunny ground—
> So without shame I spake : "I will be wise
> And just and free and mild, if in me lies
> Such power, for I grow weary to behold
> The selfish and the strong still tyrannise
> Without reproach or check." I then controlled
> My tears, my heart grew calm, and I was meek and bold.

To be wise and just and free and mild, and by the
power thus acquired to help the oppressed to shake off
the tyranny of the oppressor, this was the life-work to
which he solemnly dedicated himself—the shy, gentle,
shrinking boy who had been sent to Eton to acquire that
external polish which his parents judged to be the chief
characteristic of a gentleman.[1]

So the rapturous moments passed, and the darkness of
the school life, with its petty tyrannies and wretched

---

[1] This incident of Shelley's moral and intellectual awakening recorded in
the introductory stanzas of *Laon and Cythna*, and also alluded to in the
Hymn to Intellectual Beauty and *Julian and Maddalo*, is referred
by Dr. Dowden and all recent authorities to the period of Shelley's
school-life at Brentford, and not at Eton. I think, however, that Lady
Shelley was right when in the *Shelley Memorials* she indicated Eton as the
scene of Shelley's vow. It is in the highest degree improbable that any
boy, even such a boy as Shelley, would have experienced such emotions
before the age of twelve ; but this difficulty vanishes if we suppose the vow
to have been made at Eton, where Shelley stayed till he was eighteen. It
is significant, too, that in his letter to Godwin, dated January 10, 1812,
Shelley distinctly attributes the awakening of his moral sense to his
reading of *Political Justice ;* and there is evidence in the same letter that
he first read this book somewhere about the year 1809.

meannesses, again settled down on Shelley. But henceforth there was a brighter side to his existence; he had a hope, a faith, an object before him; and he could bear with greater constancy the trials that befell him during his passage through Eton, where it is probable that he alone of boys or masters was possessed of any enlightened love of knowledge, any thorough desire for education. Even in these early days he was an indefatigable reader; and though his course of study did not lead him in the direction of scholastic honours, he nevertheless acquired a knowledge of Greek and Latin almost by intuition, and rose steadily in the school during the six years he remained there, till he was eventually in the sixth form.

Nor was he destitute of friends, few but affectionate, won from among the mass of school-fellows who for the most part misunderstood him; and in Dr. Lind, a retired physician then living in Windsor, he found what he could find in none of the Eton masters—at once a friend and a teacher, with whom he might hold free intellectual converse without shame or fear of reproof. The child's dream of a hoary-headed alchemist who could sympathise with the feelings on which others frowned was thus realised in boyhood; and the gentle benevolence of Dr. Lind, of whom Shelley never spoke in after-life without gratitude, may suggest some serious thoughts to us, as it doubtless did to Shelley, as to the relative value of fear and love in the process of education.[1]

And now let us turn to the picture of Shelley at Oxford, where we find him entered as a member of University College in the autumn of 1810. He had at length escaped from the tedious thraldom of school life

[1] A bust of Shelley, by W. W. Story, was placed in the Upper School, at Eton, on June 1, 1904. Twenty years earlier an attempt to have Shelley recognised among Etonian "worthies" had failed; and it is said that the headmaster scouted the idea on the ground that Shelley was "a bad man."

to the comparative freedom of the University, where he enjoyed ample time for reading, writing, conversing, arguing, and following to the utmost the bent of his own inclinations. At home he was for the time on cordial, if not affectionate, terms with his father, who had learnt to look with equanimity, and perhaps with a sort of qualified admiration, on the strong tendency towards authorship which he noted, even at this early stage, as a feature of his son's character, and was even heard to speak with paternal pride of the " literary turn " and " printing freaks " of the promising youth.

It is recorded of Shelley that he often devoted sixteen hours out of the twenty-four to reading; classics and modern languages, poetry and prose, physics and meta-physics—nothing seemed to come amiss to him. When " a little man," presumably one of the college tutors, informed Shelley one morning that " he must read," the pupil was able to answer, without any scruple or hesita-tion, that " he had no objection." Day after day, with one familiar friend, he used to read or discuss all sorts of subjects, connected or not connected with the course of study, notable among these, on account of their special influence on his mind, being the essays of Locke and Hume. Moreover, he was still greatly interested in the study of chemistry; and his rooms at Oxford, as at Eton, were strewn with crucibles, phials, galvanic batteries, air-pumps, microscopes, and all the apparatus of the chemist, which continued to inspire in him a wild and lawless delight. Returning fresh from some dull and wearisome lecture on mineralogy, where a learned pedant had dis-coursed heavily " about stones," the youthful enthusiast would dilate to his wondering friend on the " mysteries of matter," and the glorious future in store for the human race when the dream of Bacon's " New Atlantis " should be realised, and the powers of nature organised and enlisted in the service of man.

But the "mysteries of mind" now began to claim a still larger share of his attention, poetry and philosophy being the two great objects to which the thoughts of this strange, self-educated youth were attracted. At first it was philosophy to which he felt the stronger inclination; and as if to verify the name bestowed on him by his Etonian school-fellows, he had already adopted the atheistic doctrines of the eighteenth-century writers.

The tone of regret employed by Shelley's apologists in regard to this early line of reading shows an inability to grasp the full meaning of his career. It is true that he was by nature an idealist; yet this initial phase of keen and trenchant scepticism was a valuable and even indispensable preparation for one whose mission was to attack the tyranny of conventional thought. Had it not been for this sharp brushing away of mystical cobwebs, Shelley's genius, always dangerously prone to metaphysical subtleties, might have lost itself, like that of Swedenborg or Coleridge, in a labyrinth of phantasies, and thus have wasted or misdirected its store of moral enthusiasm.

It is important, too, to notice that the "materialism" of which Shelley became an adherent during his residence at Oxford went hand-in-hand with a remarkable ardour in the cause of gentleness and humanity. Even as a boy in Sussex he had been keenly affected by the sight of want and suffering among the poor; and his reading of Godwin's works, by which he was profoundly moved at an early period of his life, had doubtless already set him thinking, not only on the contrast, but also on the connection, between poverty and wealth. His chivalrous intervention on behalf of the down-trodden and oppressed, whether it were a starved child or an over-driven horse, had more than once brought wonder to the mind of the more phlegmatic companion of his daily rambles round Oxford.

This chosen companion was Thomas Jefferson Hogg, the Boswell of Shelleyan biography, destined to be remembered by succeeding generations of Shelley students with mingled feelings of gratitude, amusement, and disgust.[1] By nature and disposition he was a hard-headed, cynical man of the world, regarding all sentiment and enthusiasm with a kind of tolerant contempt, and firmly convinced that the great object of life is to be prosperous, comfortable, and sarcastic. But at the time when he first met Shelley his worldly propensities were not yet fully developed, and his character was redeemed by a touch of literary taste and a love of intellectual liberty which were the chief bonds of the friendship that was soon established between the two undergraduates, one of whom was now preparing for the career of a philanthropist, the other for that of a lawyer.

The force of the influence which the shy idealist exercised over the mind of the shrewd cynic may be measured by the warmth of the praise bestowed by Hogg on Shelley in the record of their life at Oxford. which he published more than twenty years later. It was the first instance of the homage which was so often paid to Shelley's unworldly nature by such rough, busy, matter-of-fact men as chanced to be brought in contact

[1] "Apart from Shelley, Hogg was simply a rough diamond—a coarse-tongued jester, whose jokes did not improve with time; magnetised by Shelley's genius into genuine and loyal admiration of faculties the most dissimilar to his own, he was able. in spite of his seeming disqualifications, to give us, in his *Shelley at Oxford*, one of the best—perhaps the very best—of all the portraits of the poet, a portrait which, incorporated in his *Life of Shelley*, stands out in strong relief from the ineptitude and vulgarity of its surroundings." (Essay on "Hogg's Life of Shelley," by Henry S. Salt, *Shelley Society's Papers*, vol. ii.)

with it; it was, as Carlyle wrote of the devotion of the
true Boswell, "a genuine reverence for excellence; a
worship for heroes, at a time when neither heroes nor
worship were surmised to exist." But in Hogg's case
the hero-worship was further set off and enhanced by
the sense of amazement and pity aroused in his breast
at the sight of Shelley's unbusiness-like habits and
quixotic temperament. How would "his poor friend"
have fared, had not *he* been present to advise and assist
him?

Meantime those were pleasant days when the two
friends devoted the autumn afternoons to long country
rambles, and when their after-supper conversations were
prolonged until the college clock struck two. But
already, at the close of Shelley's first term at Oxford,
signs were not wanting that this happiness would be
short-lived. His father's suspicions had been aroused
on the subject of his heterodox opinions, and the
Christmas holidays spent by Shelley at Field Place were
a time of mutual distrust. Now there are some youthful
failings which may be overlooked in respectable English
households; there are others which cannot be overlooked, and unfortunately Shelley's belonged to the
latter class. If it had been merely a propensity to
gambling, swearing, drinking, or some of the other
indiscretions not uncommon among Oxford students at
that date, Mr. Timothy Shelley would perhaps not have
quite despaired of his son; but when a young man, in
all simplicity and good faith, sets himself to question
the truth of certain doctrines which he is bound to take
for granted, then it is clear that such an offender must
be disowned, until he sees the necessity of repenting.
Unhappily this was a necessity that Shelley, in spite of
his excellent education at Eton and Oxford, could not be

brought to see; and it must, I suppose, be attributed to his translunary origin that, instead of recognising the force of the parental arguments, he had the temerity to attempt himself to "illuminate" his father.

The result was as might have been foreseen by a youth of more reasonable disposition. At the end of the vacation he returned to Oxford in disfavour with both his parents, and was thrown into a restless, unhappy, and excited frame of mind. "I will crush intolerance; I will at least attempt it." Such was his spirit early in 1811, and he already hoped "to gratify some of this insatiable feeling in poetry."

In March, 1811, Shelley and Hogg, still inseparable in their studies, and eager in the pursuit of knowledge, had come to the conclusion that they must henceforth devote a still larger portion of time to their joint reading; both of them being unaware that the attention of the college authorities, which had for some time been attracted by their singularity of dress and conduct, was now centred on a small pamphlet, entitled *The Necessity of Atheism*, which Shelley had lately written and circulated, and to which Hogg had contributed a preface. With that childlike simplicity which could not, or would not, realise that learned men may be actuated by other motives than a desire to seek the truth, the youthful disputant had forwarded copies of his pamphlet to various dignitaries of the university and the Church, inviting free discussion, criticism, and, if possible, refutation, of the principles set forth.

The matter was brought to the notice of the Master and Fellows of University College, and after some previous consideration they summoned Shelley before them. The aspect of the culprit who had thus attempted to undermine the pillars of the English Church was not such as might have been expected from the desperate nature of the deed. It is true that the wildness of his long hair, and the lack of spruceness in his costume, constituted a breach of etiquette on which the authorities looked with disfavour; yet there was something in the animation of his features, the mingled firmness and gentleness of his manner, and his tall yet bent and fragile figure, that would have impressed his judges favourably, could it have been dissociated from his pernicious views. As he would neither disown the authorship of the obnoxious pamphlet, nor answer any questions on the subject, a sentence of expulsion was pronounced; and Hogg's generous intervention only resulted in his sharing the same fate.

Thus ended Shelley's experiences of the education of a gentleman. The disappointment at the time was a bitter one, and the blow was severely felt. "It would seem, indeed," wrote Hogg in his *Shelley at Oxford*, "to one who rightly considered the final cause of the institution of a university, that all the rewards, all the honours, the most opulent foundation could accumulate would be inadequate to remunerate an individual whose thirst for knowledge was so intense, and his activity in the pursuit of it so wonderful and so unwearied." Shelley certainly desired no reward for what was in him an instinct rather than an effort, but he equally little anticipated that these very qualities would bring about his disgrace.[1]

---

[1] Eighty-two years after his expulsion the authorities of University College, Oxford, mollified doubtless by the "angelic" view of Shelley's character, allowed a statue by Mr. Onslow Ford to be erected there. We should be thankful perhaps that they did not avail themselves of the suggestion rashly offered by Mr. Bernard Shaw, and decorate their walls with "a relief representing Shelley in a tall hat, Bible in hand, leading his children on Sunday morning to the church of his native parish." But it must be said that the representation of Shelley in this statue, and also in that erected at Christchurch Priory, Bournemouth, in the pathetic image of a dead and helpless figure, is essentially untrue and inappropriate. Shelley's is the poetry of life, not of death.

CHAPTER IV.

MARRIAGE WITHOUT LOVE

IT was not until the middle of May, 1811, or nearly two months after the expulsion from Oxford, that Shelley's father, finding him deaf to threats and expostulations, consented to receive him at home, and to make him a small annual allowance, with permission to live where and how he liked. On his reappearance at Field Place, Shelley was doubtless regarded by his relatives much in the light of a prodigal son, though he himself was so far from admitting that he had sinned before heaven that we find him successfully "illuminating" his uncle with the very pamphlet which had been the cause of his present troubles.[1]

Nevertheless, his position at this time was lonely and disheartening, and had not his nature, though sensitive and impressionable in the extreme, possessed also a singular faculty of hopefulness and recovery, he could hardly have persevered longer in what must have seemed a vain and useless struggle. He had long passed that point which is often reached in the early stage of independent thought, where young gentlemen may yet discover that they have made an error of judgment, and may make their way back to the fold of propriety and affluence. He had completely lost the affections of his cousin Harriet Grove, a beautiful girl to whom he had

---

[1] "I am now with my uncle. He is a very hearty fellow, and has behaved very nobly to me, in return for which I have illuminated him." (Letter to Hogg.)

been greatly attached; he had forfeited his bright prospect at the University and the goodwill of his parents. What was he to do in life, and what hope could he entertain of carrying out any of the numerous schemes on which he had set his heart? He had thought at one time of studying medicine, but that plan did not commend itself to his advisers. His father urged him to become a Whig politician, but Whiggism was not exactly congenial to Shelley's tastes.

In this restless and unsettled state he found a temporary consolation in his correspondence with his friend Hogg, who was now studying for the legal profession at York, and thither he accordingly despatched a series of letters, written in alternate moods of nervous excitement and depression. Always quick to magnify and idealise what interested and affected him, he had now conceived an exalted notion of Hogg's virtues and magnanimity, and devoted himself eagerly to the consideration of a plan for the union of that "noble being" with his sister Elizabeth.

Miss Hitchener, a Sussex schoolmistress of advanced views, whose acquaintance he had recently made, was another correspondent to whom Shelley freely unburdened his mind on controversial subjects, and whom he regarded at this time as the ideal of female excellence. Then, again, there were letters to be exchanged, chiefly on religious questions, with Miss Harriet Westbrook, a school-fellow of his sisters, to whom he had been introduced during his recent stay in London; but his interest in this correspondence did not at all equal that which he felt in the two others. Harriet Westbrook was a charming and good-natured girl; but Shelley's mind was still too full of the more beautiful Harriet Grove for him to be in any danger of again falling in love.

Yet this Westbrook family was fated within a short time to have a most powerful and malignant influence on the course of Shelley's life, and on his chances of personal happiness. Eliza Westbrook, Harriet's elder sister, a grown-up woman of unprepossessing appearance and character, was evidently interested and attracted by the young enthusiast who preached the regeneration of society and was heir to Field Place. When she invited Shelley to the house of her father, a retired hotel-keeper, and talked to him of love, and (to quote Shelley's own words) was "too civil by half," was it her sole object that Shelley and Harriet should be brought together? The exact truth about these matters will probably never be published, even if any record survives; but it can hardly be doubted that Eliza Westbrook was playing some deep game at this time, and that Harriet was a mere tool and instrument in her hands.

How could it be otherwise? Harriet was a school-girl of sixteen, pretty and pleasing in appearance and manners, but utterly destitute of any real strength of character, the mere reflex of the surroundings in which her lot was cast; at first a methodist in religious creed, and looking forward to some day marrying a minister, though at the same time confessing in her own mind that the military were the most fascinating of men— afterwards an easy convert to Shelley's revolutionary arguments. It is true that she was far from being actually illiterate; but her interest in literature was a mere passing illusion, derived at second-hand from opinions which she chanced to hear expressed. Neither in religion nor in culture had she any fixed principles or convictions which might prove a guidance and support. And though at this early age she was bright, winning, and compliant, there was a fibre of obstinacy and worldliness in her nature which was destined to make itself felt as the years went on. Philanthropic schemes, simplicity of living, and theories of universal freedom might charm her fancy for awhile, but she was not one who would endure to make sacrifices for notions which could only affect her superficially, or dedicate a lifetime to a work for which in her heart she cared not at all.

This was the girl who was corresponding with Shelley in the early summer of 1811, until in August of the same year, under stress of her father's real or pretended tyranny, she threw herself on his protection, confessed her secret affection, and so aroused the sympathy and pity of one who "if he knew anything about love was not in love," that the affair ended in their elopement and marriage.

"Foolish but generous" has been the usual verdict of Shelley's biographers regarding the marriage with Harriet, the unhappy consequences of which were apparent to the last day of his life. Let it be frankly recognised that the folly was greatly in excess of the generosity, and that we miss in this disastrous action the clear-sighted and faithful adhesion to rational principles which was conspicuous in the other great turning-points of his life. Had it not been for the restless, excited condition of his mind at this time, he would have seen, as he saw afterwards, that it could be no duty of his to devote himself to a girl whom he did not love, and of whose fitness to be his permanent companion he had by no means satisfied himself. From such a blunder there could only ensue a life-long crop of calamities, which, though insufficient to warp the main purpose of his strong and indomitable will, would yet have the power to cause him and others much acute suffering. Unfortunately, in the low state of his spirits at that time, it seemed to Shelley that "the only thing worth living for was self-sacrifice," and this self-sacrifice took the form of becoming the brother-in-law of Eliza Westbrook.

It is odd that the critics who have been at pains to rake up every fault and foible of Shelley's career should as a rule have looked complacently on this one great error of his lifetime; but no doubt their leniency is chiefly due to the tranquillising effect of the marriage service performed at Edinburgh on August 28, 1811. That Shelley himself was soon a wiser and severer judge of his own conduct is proved by the tone of his letters to Miss Hitchener in October of the same year. "In one short week," he writes, referring to his marriage with Harriet, "how changed were all my prospects. How bitterly I curse my bondage! Yet this was unavoidable."

Soon after their arrival in Edinburgh, Shelley and Harriet were joined by the admirable Hogg, in whose company they returned after a few weeks to York. There the party was further reinforced by the presence of Eliza Westbrook, who was henceforth to be a frequent inmate of Shelley's household, and to exercise complete control over Harriet in all domestic matters—an infliction which Shelley, for pecuniary reasons, was unable to resent as he might otherwise have done. It was under these auspices that Shelley, whose age was then nineteen, commenced that ardent crusade against tyranny and intolerance which in one form or another was always the main object of his life.

The sojourn at York, though short, was long enough to disillusion Shelley's mind as to the virtues of his friend Hogg, whose conduct to Harriet necessitated a sudden departure to Keswick, while the "noble being"

whose life-long companionship Shelley had so ardently
desired was left to pursue his legal duties in solitude
and remorse, and Shelley himself found material for
much sorrowful reflection in this unsuspected baseness
of his first and most trusted friend. At Keswick he
made the acquaintance of Southey, of whose writings he
had long been an admirer, and in whom he now thought
to find a kindred spirit, moved by the same passionate
enthusiasm for freedom; he found instead a kindly,
middle-aged gentleman, who could not always see the
point of a discussion, and whose " Ah, when you are as
old as I am ! " was his mainstay in argument.

Disappointed in these personal experiences, Shelley
began to turn his eyes towards the field of politics, and
his interest was naturally directed to Ireland as the
scene which illustrated most forcibly the effects of a
policy of repression.   Yet what benefit could he conceive
to have resulted from his two months' visit to Dublin
in the early part of 1812 ?   He might indeed feel
confident in his own heart of the justice and truth of
the opinions set forth in his *Address to the Irish People*,
but he could not be unaware that the publication of the
pamphlet had failed to produce the effect which he
anticipated ; nor could he foresee, by way of comfort for
temporary failure, that the history of the next half-
century would amply illustrate the essential wisdom of
his views.   At Dublin, too, as at Keswick, his youth
was much against him ; and, as if nineteen were not an
early enough age at which to begin the work of reforming the world, his Irish servant gave out that he was
only fifteen, thus throwing an increased appearance of
juvenility over an enterprise which had been undertaken
in a very serious spirit.

Moved by the remonstrances of the philosopher

Godwin, with whom he had commenced a correspondence, he withdrew from further interference in Irish
affairs, and wandered for a time through the picturesque
parts of Wales and the coast of North Devon, amusing
himself meanwhile by sending forth copies of his
Declaration of Rights, and other revolutionary docu-
ments, in floating bottles and balloons, or engaged in
the more important occupation of writing his poem
Queen Mab.

During these wanderings Shelley had been reluctantly
compelled to sacrifice another of his youthful ideals of
excellence. As he had once mistaken Hogg for the
paragon of manly virtue, so for a longer time did he
idealise his correspondent, Miss Hitchener, until she
became, to his imagination, "a mighty intellect which
may one day enlighten thousands." The addition of
her presence to Shelley's household had been looked
forward to as a blissful event; but when it had become
a reality disappointment had ensued, with the result
that his "Portia," whose genius Shelley had invoked to
stimulate his own, was induced after a few months to
return to her Sussex home, to the relief of her former
fellow-enthusiast.[1]

As he looked back over this restless period of desultory
schemes and broken ideals, Shelley's heart must sometimes have been filled with a feeling akin to despair.
His campaign against "intolerance" had failed to
produce the slightest mitigation of the evils which he
sought to cure, its only apparent result being to embitter
his relations with society, and thereby to disturb his own

[1] See *Letters from Percy Bysshe Shelley to Elizabeth Hitchener*, edited
by Bertram Dobell, 1908. "I only know one anecdote of her," says Medwin,
"which Shelley used to relate, laughing till the tears ran down his cheeks.
She perpetrated an ode, proving that she was a great stickler for the rights
of her sex, the first line of which ran thus :—
  'All, all are men—women and all.'"

security and peace of mind. His early ideals of excellence had been in some cases rudely shaken, in others entirely destroyed. If there was one plan which, above all others, had been often present in his mind after the elopement with Harriet, it was to choose some beautiful yet unpretentious home, and there, in the neighbourhood of friends and sympathisers, to dwell " for ever " and devote himself to the study of poetry and philosophy. Yet, instead of securing this blissful home of rest, he had roamed for two years from place to place, and led a life like that of the Wandering Jew whose character he was already fond of introducing in his writings. It was indeed a strange and chequered experience that had been amassed by a youth of twenty-one. Well might he point out in his *Notes to Queen Mab* that time is not to be measured only by its duration, nor length of life merely by number of years, and that " the life of a man of virtue and talent, who should die in his thirtieth year," may be, by comparison, a long one.

It was, however, in his domestic affairs that about this time Shelley began to find his chief cause for disquietude. His money troubles, the result in part of his own lavish generosity and total inability to economise, were now beginning to press heavily on his mind. But this was not the worst of his anxieties.

Hitherto his marriage with Harriet had perhaps been a happier one than its origin could have warranted him in expecting, a sincere affection having gradually grown up between them, owing in great measure to Harriet's easy good temper and ready compliance with his habits and opinions. But the seed of disunion was already sown in the fact that the revolutionary ideas which were the life and soul of his being were to Harriet nothing more than a matter of passing interest and excitement.

As she grew up to full womanhood, the true purport of her character, latent hitherto and merged in Shelley's stronger personality, was slowly but surely developed, with the result that, in addition to the disenchantment of his boyish ideals and the failure of his philanthropic crusade, it was becoming evident to Shelley that he was soon likely to lose even the consolation of sympathy and tranquillity at home. There was a trait of coldness and insensibility in Harriet's nature which was in marked contrast with the impassioned warmth of his own ; while the presence of Eliza Westbrook, at first tolerated as a necessity, was every day becoming a more insufferable burden and annoyance.

Small wonder, then, that Shelley was dejected and despondent during the days which he spent at Bracknell, for he must have felt that a sharp crisis was approaching in his fate. He was destined yet to rise to nobler efforts and wiser methods of warfare ; but first there was a valley of deep humiliation to be crossed, and a heavy penalty to be paid for the error which he had committed.

In the meantime the years had not passed without their natural pleasures and consolations. Through all the changes of his wanderings, through all his embarrassments, he had contrived to satisfy that innate love of reading and self-instruction which was to him a life-long instinct. Scarce less powerful, even at this early age, was the desire to give his own thoughts and opinions to the world. Even as a schoolboy he had found his way to the printer's, for his idealism was combined with a singularly practical disposition, in which theory went hand and hand with performance.

Among the various productions of this youthful period, the majority of which he could not but acknowledge to be failures, *Queen Mab* at any rate must have given some satisfaction to its author, who could not have been left quite in ignorance that a few sympathetic hearts had here and there been thrilled by this eloquent expression of the gospel of humanity and free thought. Whatever else he had done, or failed to do, this strange youth of one-and-twenty had penned the most notable and spirited protest of his generation against the religious bigotry which stunts the fair growth of the human intellect, and against the commercial greed which tramples out the gentler instincts of life. Never before in English poetry had the tyranny of the rich over the poor, of the strong over the weak, been so indignantly, and withal so truthfully, denounced.[1]

The enthusiasm which had inspired *Queen Mab* was a proof that Shelley possessed that happy union of sensibility and strength which alone could enable him to go through life without abating the keenness of his sympathies or withdrawing in despair from his crusade. His chief support in this darkest period of his life was to be found in the tenacity with which he still clung to his early boyish vow—to be wise and just and free.

To the comforts thus derived from a single-hearted integrity of purpose were added those of friendship. Shelley was soon reconciled to his old college comrade; and though their intimacy could never be restored on the former confident footing, Hogg was a frequent and welcome visitor, both at Bracknell and in London. In

[1] I cannot follow Mr. Forman's example of relegating *Queen Mab* to the *juvenilia*, as if it were unworthy of the serious attention of Shelley students. It is in many ways a crude and ill-considered performance, but its defects lie more in the style than in the conception—to repeat what Shelley said of it in later years, "the matter is good, but the treatment is not equal." The views expressed in *Queen Mab* on religious and social topics are practically the same as those held by Shelley to the last day of his life, and, as Mr. Forman himself tells us, "the poem and its notes have played a considerable part in the growth of freethought in England and America, especially among the working classes." For both of these reasons it seems to me that *Queen Mab* will always maintain an honourable place in the records of its author's achievements.

Thomas Love Peacock, the novelist, a man of more literary and cultured tastes than Hogg, but fully as sarcastic and cynical, Shelley had lately made another friend—an equally striking illustration of the singular attraction which he could exercise on minds of a wholly alien cast from his own. By this time, too, the correspondence with William Godwin had led to a personal acquaintance, and Shelley frequently enjoyed the conversation of the philosopher whose moral and political writings had so profoundly influenced him.

Yet another friendship in which he found a solace was that of the Newtons and Boinvilles, two families whose gentle and refined tastes were in close accord with his own, and stimulated him in the direction of that simple vegetarian diet to which he had long been inclined, and which he had now actually adopted. To such confirmed mockers and *bon vivants* as Peacock and Hogg the principles of the humane diet were necessarily unintelligible, and it must often have been a relief to Shelley to turn from their pointless witticisms to the congenial society where he met with a more liberal and sympathetic intelligence.[1]

The marriage with Harriet was the one great flaw in Shelley's otherwise consistent career. Not, of course, because it was a misalliance which alienated his friends and ruined his worldly " prospects "; still less because he undertook a legal responsibility when no such step could have been demanded of him, and when, by acting as ordinary youths would have done, he might have avoided all the odium that he afterwards incurred. Had Shelley

[1] Mark Twain, in his "Defence of Harriet Shelley," *North American Review*, July, 1894, speaks of the Boinville family as " an unwholesome prairie dog's nest," the insinuation being that Shelley was carrying on an intrigue with Mrs. Boinville's daughter Cornelia. There is no ground whatever for this suggestion, as may be seen by a statement of the facts in Dowden's Life of Shelley.

been merely a " gentleman," or that other dismal product of civilisation, a " man of the world," he might justly be charged with folly in thus showing consideration for the honour of an innkeeper's daughter.   But, as the case stands, the error committed by him was simply that of allying himself with a woman whom he did not love. Love was the supreme instinct of Shelley's nature, the beacon-light which guided him safely through the stormy sea of his life ; but here, at this one crisis, he rashly pledged himself in its default.   The fatal characteristic of the marriage with Harriet was that it was marriage without love.

On the other hand, it can at least be pleaded, in extenuation of a blunder which darkened Shelley's life, that, of all earthly snares and perils to which a visitor from another planet may conceivably be liable, there is nothing half so formidable as the present confused relations of the sexes—that morass of misunderstanding by whose flickering will-o'-the-wisps even a genuine lover may be deceived.   That he did not love Harriet was felt by Shelley himself ; yet, the first false step being taken, he was compelled, in his generous desire to remove a hateful stigma from the woman who trusted him, to commit himself further and further to a fatal course— the alliance with one who could never be in any real sense his partner.   There is a terrible significance in his after-references to this period :—

> Nay, was it I who wooed thee to this breast
> Which, like a serpent, thou envenomest
> As in repayment of the warmth it lent ?
> Didst thou not seek me for thine own content ?
> Did not thy love awaken mine ? [1]

Towards the end of the year 1813 grave dissensions

---

[1] *Julian and Maddalo.*

had arisen between Shelley and Harriet; and he was now face to face with the alternative of living on in a state of continual domestic disagreement, or of cutting the knot of his own troubles, and not less, as he might well believe, of Harriet's, by a bold and decisive step. " The institutions and opinions of all ages and countries have admitted in various degrees the principle of divorce." So wrote Shelley in his Chancery paper three years later ; and the desire to obtain release, practically if not legally, from this matrimonial bondage must certainly have existed in his mind in the spring of 1814, although for his children's sake he was even then willing to be nominally bound.[1]

If so many persons of ordinary temperament have found it an almost intolerable burden to be yoked throughout life to an unsympathetic companion, we can judge what a death-in-life such an existence must have been to Shelley, whose quick and emotional disposition the more eagerly craved rest and sympathy at home in proportion to the acuteness of his struggle against the outer world. " In looking back to this marriage," says his cousin and biographer, Medwin, " it is surprising, not that it should have ended in a separation, but that for so long a time he should have continued to drag on a chain, every link of which was a protraction of torture."

It might, indeed, have been foretold that a girl who always looked " as if she had just that moment stepped out of a glass case " could not be a fit companion for him ; but though Shelley, as I have said, must himself bear the blame of having married one whom he did not love, and whose character he had not rightly fathomed,

---

[1] The object of the second marriage, performed in London in March, 1814, was simply to establish the legitimacy of his child, as the validity of the Scotch marriage was open to question.

he might be pardoned for not foreseeing that Harriet's easy good-temper would be replaced, as the years went on, by a mood of hardness and insensibility. For, through all the conflicting and perplexing records of this period, it is evident that it was Harriet and not Shelley who took up an attitude of deliberate coldness and estrangement. When we seek to go a step further, and to inquire into the precise origin of the discord and the reason of Harriet's inflexibility, we find the whole subject shrouded in a mystery, which none of Shelley's biographers have been able, or willing, to dispel.

It is worth noting, however, that in his poem of *Julian and Maddalo* Shelley himself left a sketch of a character—that of a deserted and distracted lover—which was certainly meant to be an idealised record of this passage of his life, though the true import of the poem has been generally overlooked.[1] We naturally wonder if the real history of Shelley's first marriage could have furnished material for the shuddering reminiscence and tragic horror of which this part of *Julian and Maddalo* is full. Those who read between the lines can see indications of the existence of some still graver breach of sympathy between Shelley and Harriet than such as could be accounted for by mere divergence of tastes, or by that conviction of his wife's infidelity which Shelley, rightly or wrongly, entertained to the end. In the statement drawn up at the time of the Chancery suit, Shelley thus alluded to his parting from Harriet: "Delicacy forbids me to say more than that we were disunited by incurable dissensions."

[1] The subject was fully treated by me in an essay on *Julian and Maddalo*, read before the Shelley Society in 1888, and published in the Society's Papers, Part II., some sentences of which are reproduced in this chapter. I may mention that I received, through Dr. Furnivall, a message from Robert Browning to the effect that from the first appearance of *Julian and Maddalo* he had held the view above stated, though he would not press it in detail.

At any rate, this was Shelley's position in the early months of 1814. There was a hopeless lack of sympathy between himself and his wife, but the barrier that separated them was not of his making; for however great the measure of his folly in allowing himself to be entrapped into the disastrous marriage, his conscience acquitted him of any guilt in his after-conduct towards Harriet, who now coldly rejected all offers of reconciliation.[1] What, then, was he to do? Was he to drag on a weary existence until death should relieve him or his wife from their loveless union? In the opinion of the orthodox he was bound to do this; but in his own opinion, as expressed in his *Notes to Queen Mab*, the opposite course was far more in accordance with genuine morality. "A husband and wife," he had written, "ought to continue so long united as they love each other."

Conscientiously holding these views, he looked upon his marriage with Harriet as already at an end. To his protection, support, and assistance she was still, and would always be, entitled; but their closer union would henceforth be as irrevocably dissolved as if the divorce court had pronounced a formal decree of separation.

---

[1] See the poem "To Harriet," May, 1814.

CHAPTER V.

LOVE WITHOUT MARRIAGE

IT was at this darkest moment of his destiny that Shelley first became acquainted with Mary Godwin, whose life and fortunes were so soon to be indissolubly blended with his own. Her father, William Godwin, had long exercised a moderating, and on the whole beneficial, influence on the mind of his youthful admirer; and Shelley, on his part, had done, and was doing, his utmost to assist Godwin in the pecuniary troubles which embittered his declining years. The philosopher and the poet were thus drawn somewhat closely together when Shelley was in London in the early part of 1814.

In this way an intimacy arose between Shelley and Mary, then in her seventeenth year, the daughter of the famous Mary Wollstonecraft, Godwin's first wife; and the friendship thus formed soon ripened into love—a love, be it remembered, which was not a cause but a consequence of Shelley's estrangement from Harriet.[1]

It would be well if those who pass judgment on Shelley and Mary for their conduct at this crisis could bring themselves to view the facts from the standpoint of the parties concerned, and to remember that both Shelley

[1] This is proved beyond question by the impartial evidence of dates. There was, as Professor Dowden shows, a "deep division" between Shelley and Harriet early in 1814, whereas Shelley was unacquainted with Mary until May or June of the same year. It is therefore idle to assert that Shelley's quarrel with Harriet was the outcome of a newer fancy or "affinity." Indeed, this is admitted by some writers who blame Shelley for his "failure of love" towards Harriet. "He would never have fallen in love with Mary," says Mr. Clutton-Brock, "unless he had been out of love with Harriet."

and Mary, and indeed Harriet also, belonged to that not inconsiderable class who see in the marriage-bond nothing more than a human institution, devoid of moral sanctity. Shelley's union with Harriet being practically, though not legally, at an end, neither he nor Mary could reasonably be blamed for not conforming to a standard of ethics from which they conscientiously dissented. It was in no reckless or immoral spirit, but with a deep conviction of the essential innocence of their act, that they plighted their love as they stood by Mary Wollstonecraft's grave in the old St. Pancras's churchyard. As the spot was full of sacred memories, so the vow there made was full of solemn and loyal intent.

> Alas, that love should be a blight and snare
> To those who seek all sympathies in one!
> Such once I sought in vain; then black despair,
> The shadow of a starless night, was thrown
> Over the world in which I moved alone:
> Yet never found I one not false to me,
> Hard hearts, and cold, like weights of icy stone,
> Which crushed and withered mine, that could not be
> Aught but a lifeless clog, until revived by thee.
>
> Thou Friend, whose presence on my wintry heart
> Fell like bright Spring upon some herbless plain,
> How beautiful and calm and free thou wert
> In thy young wisdom, when the mortal chain
> Of Custom thou didst burst and rend in twain,
> And walked as free as light the clouds among,
> Which many an envious slave then breathed in vain
> From his dim dungeon, and my spirit sprung
> To meet thee from the woes which had begirt it long.[1]

On July 28, some two or three weeks after this event, Shelley and Mary left England for the Continent. About the middle of the preceding month Harriet had gone to live with her father and sister at Bath; and before his

---

[1] From the Dedication of *Laon and Cythna*.

departure from England, Shelley, after a final interview, had been careful to provide that she should be in no want of money. If there was one crime of which he was by his very nature incapable, it was that of a cruel and selfish desertion; and he therefore appears to have had no sort of apprehension that in thus deliberately separating himself from his wife he would incur the odious charge of having deserted her. With all his early experience, he had yet to realise that slander is the most effective weapon of bigotry, and that the respectability which can look complacently on marriage without love can never forgive the practice of love without marriage.

It was a strange party that started from Godwin's house in the early dawn of that memorable summer morning—Shelley, with his eager eyes and wild spiritual expression; Mary, even at that early age, calm and sedate in manner, and noticeable for her fair hair and high, tablet-like forehead; and Godwin's step-daughter, Claire Clairmont, a lively, quick-eyed brunette, whose whim it was to accompany the fugitives in their adventures.

To baffle pursuit by driving in a post-chaise to Dover; to cross the Channel in an open boat at the imminent risk of their lives, to purchase an ass at Paris, on whose back to ride in turn during the journey to Switzerland; to despatch a letter to Harriet with a suggestion, made in all sincerity and good faith, that she too should join the party as a friend and guest;[1] to hire a house for six months on the shore of the lake of Lucerne, and then to

[1] This letter, according to Matthew Arnold's pronouncement, was "precisely the letter which a man in the writer's circumstances should not have written." Regarded from the orthodox standpoint, this is undoubtedly true; yet the letter, otherwise regarded, was a most natural and Shelleyan one, and might almost be employed as a test of a real understanding of Shelley's elemental character. He considered his marital relations with Harriet to be finally at an end; nevertheless, he desired still to assist and befriend her, and was not in the least likely to be debarred from making what he thought a kindly suggestion, by the knowledge (for he knew it as well as anyone else) that the offer was an unusual one.

leave it after two days' sojourn; to travel homewards in public boats and fragile canoes down the Reuss and the Rhine; and to reach England with scarcely a crown in their purse after their "six weeks' tour"—these were a few of the incidents in what was perhaps the strangest and most romantic honeymoon ever vouchsafed by guardian sprites to mortal lovers.

But the months that followed this brief dream of happiness were like those that had preceded it, a time of trouble and anxiety; and it may be doubted if Shelley could ever have fought his way through the dreary close of this most trying year had he not now been cheered by the sympathy of a gifted woman. This alone could compensate him for the changed looks of shocked and alienated friends; for the coldness of Godwin, who bitterly resented the step his daughter had taken; for the accumulation of debts and the persecution of duns, which rendered life in London almost unbearable towards the end of the year; and, above all, for the pain of the occasional interviews with Harriet, whom he still continued to visit and advise.

Yet, in spite of the many trials which had to be undergone during this period, Shelley's alliance with Mary Godwin was nothing less to him than the beginning of a new moral and intellectual life. It was not merely that through Mary's companionship his mind, which was always delicately balanced between hopefulness and despondency, was filled with reviving hope; but henceforth, partly from the experience gained in the past, and partly from the more stimulating influence of his new surroundings, he entered on a larger and fuller existence, with wider views of man and nature, and more wisdom in his manner of promoting the doctrines which he had so deeply at heart. Very important, too, in the strong impression left on his mind, and powerfully affecting his subsequent writings, was his recent visit, in the six weeks' tour, to the mighty mountains and rivers of the Continent; for the first sight of the Alps and the Rhine were to him a new revelation of the holiness and majesty of Nature.

With the opening of the new year Shelley was relieved from the pressing pecuniary cares by which he had so long been harassed. At the death of his grandfather, Sir Bysshe, in January, 1815, he became the immediate heir to the estates, and henceforth received an annual income of £1,000. He had, moreover, the option of largely increasing the property to which he would succeed on his father's death by agreeing to a perpetual entail; but he refused this, as he had refused a similar offer three years previously, on the ground that he could not fairly and conscientiously entail so great a "command over labour" on those who might use the power thus given for purposes of oppression.

In the summer and autumn of 1815 we see him settled awhile at Bishopsgate, on the border of Windsor Forest, and within reach of the Thames, where he enjoyed a period of greater tranquillity than had hitherto fallen to his lot. Yet it is noticeable that a tone of melancholy pervades most of his writings of this date; his sufferings, physical and mental, had seriously undermined his health, and in the early months of this year the danger of consumption had compelled him to look death closely in the face. A sorrowful reminiscence, a sense of despondency left from past troubles, thus gave a slightly morbid tinge to work which was in reality done under circumstances of unusual restfulness and prosperity;[1] but this dejection was soon to pass away,

[1] *E.g.*, in his poem *Alastor*, written under the oaks of Windsor Forest.

together with the particular symptoms of ill-health in which it originated. The close of Shelley's and Mary's stay at Bishopsgate was made memorable to them by the birth of their son William, the "delightful child" to whom some of his most beautiful verses were afterwards dedicated.

At the approach of the next summer, Shelley and Mary, again accompanied by Claire Clairmont, started on a second visit to Switzerland, and there spent three months in the neighbourhood of Geneva. Here they became closely associated with Byron, with whom Claire, unknown to her friends, had already formed an acquaintance in London during the previous year. Both Byron and Shelley were exiles from their native land, but except for this bond of union there was little in common between them—the one a professed cynic, a votary of pride and scepticism, the other a believer in the perfectibility of man and the gospel of gentleness and love.

"In the forehead and head of Byron," says Gilfillan, in his notable description, "there was a more massive power and breadth; Shelley's had a smooth, arched, spiritual expression; wrinkles there seemed none on his brow; it was as if perpetual youth had there dropped its freshness. Byron's eye seemed the focus of lust and pride; Shelley's was mild, pensive, fixed on you, but seeing through the mist of its own idealism. Defiance curled Byron's nostril, and sensuality steeped his full, large lips; the lower portions of Shelley's face were frail, feminine, and flexible. Byron's head was turned upwards, as if, having proudly risen above his contemporaries, he were daring to claim kindred or to demand a contest with a superior order' of beings; Shelley's was half bent in reverence and humility before some vast vision seen by his eye alone. In the portrait of Byron, taken at the age of nineteen, you see the unnatural age of premature passion; his hair is grey, his dress is youthful, but his face is old. In Shelley you see the eternal child, none the less because the hair is grey, and that sorrow seems half his immortality."

It might well have been thought that Byron, the haughty misanthrope, would scorn the gentle idealist whose creed appeared to him so visionary. But this was not the case; for Byron discovered in Switzerland what he again realised two years later at Venice, that there was a strength and sincerity in Shelley's nature— "genius joined to simplicity" was his own expression— which was quite unlike anything he had seen in other men, and against which he felt neither inclination nor power to employ the shafts of his deadly sarcasm and invective. It was not Byron's habit to be too sparing or scrupulous in his remarks on friend or foe; but it is said that against Shelley he never uttered a word of detractation; while in their personal intercourse he treated his opinion with marked and unusual deference. It was a notable tribute of admiration and respect, paid almost unconsciously by a proud and faulty spirit to one whom he secretly felt to be his superior. "If people only appreciated Shelley, where should *I* be?" was Byron's remark; and the words spoken playfully at the time of utterance have much significance when looked back to by later generations of readers.

Meantime the two poets, unlike in all else, but allies in their revolt against the formalities of society, spent many long days together in the region which Rousseau's genius had immortalised. Water excursions by day, in which Shelley gratified to the full that passion for boating which he had already acquired on the Thames, and the telling of ghost-stories by night, from which originated Mary Shelley's novel *Frankenstein*, made the time pass pleasantly enough, until Shelley and Mary returned to England in September.

Then again, as after their six weeks' tour in 1814, there awaited them a period of calamity, two heavy blows falling in rapid succession. The first of these was the suicide of Fanny Imlay (known as Fanny Godwin in her step-father's household), the daughter of Mary Wollstone-craft by a previous marriage, and therefore the half-sister of Mary Shelley. Her gentle and unselfish disposition had endeared her greatly to Shelley as well as to Mary, and her death was long a severe grief to him, not to be obliterated even by the still heavier shock that was to follow, when he learnt that Fanny's suicide had been followed by that of Harriet. At the very time when Shelley was searching for her in London, Harriet, in a fit of remorseful desperation at the state to which she had sunk, had drowned herself in the Serpentine, thus realising in sad earnest a suicidal purpose of which she had been in the habit of speaking often in girlhood.

It was a dark and terrible ending to that ill-omened marriage for which Shelley was in part, though not wholly, to blame ; but unless we are prepared to assert that a single rash and foolish act brings responsibility for the whole train of consequences that result therefrom, we cannot fix the guilt on Shelley's head for the con-clusion of the tragedy. In the whole matter of the separation from Harriet he had acted conscientiously, deliberately, and with due regard for Harriet's interests as well as his own. He had sacrificed his own wish to keep the two children, out of deference to her earnest entreaty that they should be left with her ; he had placed her in the hands of her nearest relatives, had visited her from time to time, and made her an ample pecuniary provision, which secured her from all want.

Cruelly, then, though he felt the shock of this death, which, as Leigh Hunt said, "tore his being to pieces," his own conscience acquitted him of any sense of guilt. "I am innocent," he solemnly declared in a letter written four years later, " of ill either done or intended ; the consequences you allude to flowed in no respect from me."

It is obvious that the maxim *De mortuis nil nisi bonum* has been stretched to the utmost in the case of Harriet Shelley, and that there has been an excessive tendency to overlook the fact that " too inexorable a forbearance with regard to one dead person would oftentimes effectually close the door to the vindication of another."[1] Let Shelley take his just share of the blame, whatever that may be ; but let us not be so hypocritical as to pretend that the conduct of Harriet after the separation throws no light on the disputes by which the separation was caused.

At the time, however, the very peculiarity of the circumstances, which precluded all chance of inquiry or explanation, placed Shelley's character at the mercy of every foe ; and so good an opportunity for blasting the fame of one who was in revolt against society was not likely to be lost. Hence arose the commonly received tale that Shelley, by his shameless immorality and cruel desertion, had caused the death of an innocent and affectionate wife. But now, in the fuller light and with the increased knowledge of a later period, it is impossible to look into the real facts of the case, as distinguished from the supposed facts, without seeing that they entirely invalidate a verdict which originated in ignorance and prejudice, and has been maintained by the same means.

For in the first place it is not true that Shelley tired of Harriet, with the fickleness attributed to him, because he chanced to meet a new attraction in Mary. Nothing

[1] De Quincey.

is more certain than that the possibility of concord between Shelley and Harriet was utterly lost before Mary had ever come upon the scene; moreover, it clearly appears that it was Harriet and not Shelley who was mainly responsible for the disagreement.

Secondly, it is not true that Shelley "deserted" Harriet or left her without due provision. She had practically deserted him and made his home intolerable before his eyes had ever rested on Mary, though undoubtedly, when it was too late, her jealousy was aroused at the new connection formed by him.

Thirdly, Harriet's death was in no sense due to any action, or neglect of action, by Shelley; but partly to the degradation of the life to which she deliberately subjected herself, and partly to a morbid nature constitutionally prone to suicide.

It is necessary to state these things plainly, because even to the present day there exists the grossest misapprehension of the facts and dates of the tragedy. It is quite fair that those who regard the marriage-tie as sacred should condemn Shelley for his breach of it; but the assertion that he stands convicted of hardness and inhumanity in his treatment of Harriet is one which must be met with instant and unhesitating denial. It is not too much to say that numbers of men who have been separated from their wives, and have yet retained the respect of respectable society, have acted with far less than Shelley's gentleness and consideration. As Leigh Hunt says:—

> Let the collegiate refusers of argument, and the conventional sowers of their wild oats, with myriads of unhappy women behind them, rise up in judgment against him! Honester men will not be hindered from doing justice to sincerity wherever they find it; nor be induced to blast the memory of

a man of genius and benevolence for one painful passage in his life, which he might have avoided had he been no better than his calumniators.[1]

Of recent years certain writers have conceived a marked distaste for what they have styled "the Harriet problem." They had no scruple whatever in utilising on every opportunity a false story as a means of blackening Shelley's name; but when once it began to appear that the facts might wear another aspect they were smitten with a sudden aversion for the controversy which they had themselves provoked! Well, if they are indeed so weary of "chatter about Shelley" (and no one will deny that he has been the subject of unnecessary, as well as necessary, contention), the remedy is in their own hands. Let *them* cease to calumniate, and *we* shall cease to explain.

[1] *Autobiography*, 1860, p. 259.

Chapter VI.

"THE HERMIT OF MARLOW"

On the outskirts of the town of Great Marlow there is a small quaint-looking house, with an inscription on the outside to commemorate the fact that Percy Bysshe Shelley there "lived and wrote." Here, during the greater part of 1817, dwelt Shelley and Mary with their son William, and here another child, a daughter, was born in September. Claire Clairmont, with her infant daughter Allegra, was again an inmate of their household.

Shelley and Mary had been married at the close of the preceding year, and, though their own union of hearts had already been complete, the ceremony, " so magical in its effects," as Shelley wrote of it, was instrumental in bringing about a reconciliation with Godwin and other alienated friends.

> Now has descended a serener hour,
> And with inconstant fortune friends return.

Thus at last Shelley was able to secure a less interrupted spell of thinking, reading, and writing; and the time spent at Marlow was one of the most important periods of his life, a year of mingled happiness and sorrow, made memorable by the beginning of life-long friendships, and by the creation of great and characteristic works in poetry and prose. At no other time did he enjoy such free scope for carrying his ideals into effect, and for giving expression to his opinions on public policy. He was never more active, more enthusiastic, than during this final year of his residence in England.

Early in March, 1817, the good people of Marlow were shocked by the news that Albion House was tenanted by a strange family who were rumoured to have announced an impious determination never to go to church. All sorts of reports were quickly current about Mr. Shelley's antecedents, and these were in great measure confirmed, shortly after his arrival, by the news that, at the instance of the relatives of his former wife, he had been deprived of the custody of her two children, no less eminent a personage than Lord Chancellor Eldon having declared Mr. Shelley's conduct to have incapacitated him for the duty of taking charge of his own offspring. Much interest was excited in the quiet little town by the advent of this unprincipled young man, and some surprise was doubtless expressed that such respectable inhabitants as Mr. Peacock and Mr. Madocks should tolerate the acquaintance of one who, as it was sometimes darkly whispered, had come to Marlow with the purpose of keeping a seraglio.

The appearance, however, of the new-comer did not convey the impression of any extreme wickedness to those who watched him, as he hurriedly returned, barethroated, and sometimes bare-headed, from his expeditions to wood or river ; indeed, there were some who saw a singular and striking benignity in his firm yet gentle manner, and eyes bright and wild as those of a deer. The lady, too, by whom he was often accompanied, seemed fair and innocent and young. Moreover, his extreme kindness to the distressed lace-makers of Marlow, and his instant generosity to those who claimed his help, soon created a reaction in his favour—at any

rate among the poorer classes of the town. It was
doubtless felt that one who had been seen to come home
bare-footed, having given his shoes to a poor woman
whom he had met limping along the road, could not be
altogether wicked, however gravely the parson might
shake his head. " Every spot is sacred that he visited,"
so wrote an inhabitant of Marlow forty years after
Shelley's sojourn there; and the words are a worthy
testimony to the unselfishness of his disposition and
the impression left by his frank and gracious benevolence.

The decision of Lord Eldon in the Chancery suit, by
which the Westbrooks had succeeded in depriving Shelley
of the care of his daughter Ianthe and his son Charles,
was perhaps the heaviest blow of all that he had to bear
on account of his heretical opinions. It was a subject
on which he could not easily trust himself to speak even
to his nearest and dearest friends.[1] But when the judgment of the court had been delivered, and the wretched
suspense of the preceding weeks was at an end, he sought
and found the best and surest consolation in those literary
labours to which he was ever eager to devote himself,
and forgot his private sorrows in his anxiety for the
welfare of a cause.

The state of the English poor during the early years
of the nineteenth century, and especially after the conclusion of the war in 1815, was in many ways pitiable;
and Shelley, with his keen sympathies, clear intellect, and

[1] Whatever we may think of the tyranny and inhumanity of Lord Eldon's
judgment, it should be observed that he stated with extreme clearness
what many later critics have failed to recognise—the deliberateness of
Shelley's actions. " This is a case in which, as the matter appears to me,
the father's principles cannot be misunderstood; in which his conduct,
which I cannot but consider as highly immoral, has been established in
proof, and established as the effect of those principles; conduct, nevertheless, which he represents to himself and others not as conduct to be
considered as immoral, but to be recommended and observed in practice,
and as worthy of approbation."

strong sense of justice, was the last man to shut his eyes
to the true causes of social distress, as several anecdotes
recorded by Hogg and other friends testify very distinctly.
When he adopted the doctrines of Godwin's *Political
Justice*, and gave new expression to the same in his own
Notes to Queen Mab, he did this in no spirit of mere
boyish bravado, but with a clear conviction from which
he never afterwards swerved, although his views on the
subject of property obtained him more ill-will, according
to his biographer, Medwin, than any other of his
heresies.

In the two political pamphlets which he published
during his residence at Marlow he reverted to these
social questions of which he had treated in *Queen Mab ;*
and though he had now outgrown the errors of style from
which his youthful poem was not free, he could conscientiously assert that his opinions had been strengthened
and confirmed by the experience that the years had
brought him.   However statesmen might temporise and
learned economists split straws, in their partiality for the
established order of things, one writer at any rate, the
despised and calumniated " Hermit of Marlow," went to
the root of the matter in his plea for justice and freedom,
when he asserted that the luxuries and comforts of the rich
are a tax on the industry of the poor.   But while thus
insisting on the supreme importance of the social question, Shelley was in other respects an ardent upholder
of the program of political reform, as advocated by Leigh
Hunt and the Radical party of the day.

It was in poetry, however, and not in prose, that
Shelley did his chief work at Marlow.   For now it was
that he wrote *Laon and Cythna*, his epic of free thought
and free love, in which the revolutionary ideas advanced
in *Queen Mab* were still further developed, and the

doctrine of human perfectibility, adopted from Godwin, was set forth in narrative form. In the character of Cythna, the heroine of the story, we have Shelley's ideal of woman—the free, equal, fearless companion of man, no longer the dupe of religious superstition, but saving and cherishing all that is innocent and beautiful in life by her message of liberty and love.

It is no wonder that Shelley, with his lofty conception of woman's nature and the holiness of her mission, should have been, by a sort of magnetic attraction, an object of interest and affection to all women with whom he became acquainted. We are told by Hogg (who, it may be surmised, was the more impressed by the treatment Shelley received owing to the contrast afforded by his own) that, from the moment the poet entered a house, he excited the liveliest and warmest solicitude of all female inmates from the highest to the lowest, and that "he was often called by names of endearment as Ariel, Oberon, and spoken of by the ladies of his acquaintance as the Elfin King, the King of Faery, and under other affectionate titles." And it is certain that the fantastic traits in Shelley's youthful character had not been obliterated by the maturer qualities of philanthropist and poet; for the hermit of Marlow was still essentially the same person as the dreamy child of Field Place.

> He took strange caprices [says the same friend and biographer], unfounded frights and dislikes, vain apprehensions and panic terrors, and therefore he absented himself from formal and sacred engagements. He was unconscious and oblivious of times, places, persons, and seasons; and falling into some poetic vision, some day-dream, he quickly and completely forgot all that he had repeatedly and solemnly promised; or he ran away after some object of imaginary urgency and importance, which suddenly came into his head, setting off in vain pursuit of it he knew not whither.

At Marlow he would sometimes playfully account for these strange absences and disappearances by saying that he had been raising the devil in Bisham woods; and the simple country folk might be pardoned for believing that there was something unearthly about this solitary haunter of waters and woodland places, when even some of his intimate friends felt a strong suspicion that he came from another planet.

It was known, too, that to escape an unwelcome visitor, or any of the wearisome ordinances of what mortals call "society," he did not hesitate to leap through an open window, or sit a whole day with barricaded doors; since, as he himself expressed it, he was not wretch enough to "tolerate" a mere acquaintance. But there was some society of which he never tired—that of children, for instance, with whom he was at once and always in sympathy, and especially that of the few congenial friends who frequently visited him. First and foremost among these was the warm-hearted Leigh Hunt, who was linked to Shelley by a bond of true and lasting friendship; Peacock, Hogg, and Godwin were also visitors at Marlow; and at Leigh Hunt's house at Hampstead he became acquainted with Hazlitt, Keats, and Horace Smith, for the last-named of whom he conceived a sincere affection.[1]

Yet, dear as his friends were, there were times when, like all other men of great and original genius, Shelley felt a sense of loneliness and despondency. It had been

[1] The charge of fickleness in friendship, so often brought against Shelley, is disproved by the simple fact that to the last day of his life he remained true to those who called him friend—Leigh Hunt, Peacock, Hogg, Medwin, Williams, Trelawny. Such coldness as arose between Shelley and Byron was certainly not the fault of the former, and it is admitted that his treatment of Godwin was patient and considerate in the extreme. The case of Miss Hitchener, the "brown demon," is the one usually cited by Shelley's critics. She, however, was not a personal friend, but a correspondent whose character Shelley, then a boy of twenty, absurdly idealised, until experience dissolved the illusion.

so at Field Place, at Eton, at Oxford, and during the period of his first marriage ; and it was destined to be the same to the end. An Ariel cannot readily be comprehended by ordinary mortals, even though he preach the gospel of love, and live according to its strictest precepts and commandments.

For Shelley gave expression to his doctrines in practice no less than in theory. Simplicity of living was an essential feature of the creed which asserted that " all men are called to participate in the community of nature's gifts." To rise early ; to spend the mornings in study, the evenings in social converse ; to write his poems as he drifted in his boat or sat in some leafy haunt ; to walk now and then in Peacock's company from Marlow to London, a distance of over thirty miles ; to live frugally and healthily on a diet from which flesh and wine were excluded—such was his course of life during the year which he spent at Marlow.

It seems a matter for regret that his stay there could not have been further prolonged ; but towards the end of 1817 a variety of reasons determined him and Mary to make another change of residence early in the new year. The chief cause of their desertion of a home which they had once thought would be permanent was probably their fear that their children, William and Clara, might be taken from them by another high-handed act of law ; for they had learnt by bitter experience that " in this extraordinary country," as Leigh Hunt expressed it, " any man's children may be taken from him to-morrow, who holds a different opinion from the Lord Chancellor in faith and morals." They also wished to go to a warmer climate for the sake of Shelley's health, and, by withdrawing for a time to a more secluded region, to be able to curtail their expenses, which had been rendered heavy of late by the too numerous loans to friends and relatives ; while a further object was to aid Claire Clairmont in taking her child Allegra to Byron.

After much consideration it was decided that all these conditions would be best fulfilled by a journey to Italy.

Chapter VII.

EXILE IN ITALY

WITH the exception of a visit to Byron at Venice in the autumn of 1818, of which a poetical record is found in *Julian and Maddalo*, Shelley's first year in Italy was a time of comparative loneliness; his position was, in fact, almost that of an exile, outlawed successively from the goodwill of his family, his university, and his native land. Accompanied by Claire Clairmont, whose daughter was transferred to Byron's charge soon after their arrival in Italy, Shelley and Mary visited Milan, Rome, Naples, and other cities, but could find no congenial resting-place such as they had found at Marlow. The winter, which was spent at Naples, left Shelley in a state of unusual dejection and despondency, as expressed by him in the well-known stanzas :—

> Alas ! I have nor hope nor health,
>   Nor peace within, nor calm around,
> Nor that content surpassing wealth
>   The sage in meditation found,
> And walked with inward glory crowned—
>   Nor fame, nor power, nor love, nor leisure,
> Others I see whom these surround—
>   Smiling they live and call life pleasure ;
> To me that cup has been dealt in another measure.

His infant daughter had died in the preceding autumn, and at Naples there died also, if report be true, a certain mysterious and enamoured lady who had made avowal of her love for the author of *Queen Mab* on the eve of his departure for Switzerland in 1816, and had since followed him from place to place with faithful but hopeless affection.

Such anecdotes as this (with various secret perils, attempted assassinations, and strange occurrences of which the authenticity can neither be proved nor disproved) must be classed among the apocrypha rather than the history of Shelley's life; but they at least indicate the sense of romance with which that life was surrounded, and the inclination of even his intimate friends to regard him as an incomprehensible being, scarcely subject to the usual laws of space and time, of whom many things might be credited which are held to be incredible in the case of ordinary men.

Very real, unhappily, was the blow which overtook Shelley and Mary on their visit to Rome in the following year; for in the early summer their only remaining child, William, died of a fever. This crowning sorrow, coming at a time when Shelley regarded himself, not without reason, as "hunted by calamity," "an exile and a Pariah," who could name at the most five individuals to whom he did not appear a prodigy of crime, might well have been expected to put an end to all his literary aspirations. But it was not so; for the indomitable spirit which had carried him through the Chancery suit, by which he had suffered an even heavier loss—the loss inflicted by the tyranny of man being more grievous than that dealt by the mysterious laws of nature—did not desert him now. The life in Italy, lonely, unhappy, almost desultory though it had hitherto been, was nevertheless acting like the summer warmth to ripen and bring to maturity the thoughts that were germinating in his mind; and the year 1819 accordingly witnessed the creation of his most characteristic and triumphant works. It was not as an idle wanderer that Shelley had become familiar with the aspect of Alps and Apennines, with the Italian sky and the Italian waters, and with the glories of such cities as Milan, Venice, Naples, Rome. The land of ideal scenery could not fail to foster and stimulate the most idealistic genius with which poet was ever endowed. Now were written the best and most vivid of the letters from Italy, which for richness of colour, combined with grace and naturalness of expression, have never been surpassed by those of any Englishman who has taken up his pen in a foreign land to describe what he saw and felt; now, too, was written the great tragedy of *The Cenci*, pre-eminently the most remarkable of modern English dramas. But the chief production of this period, and indeed of Shelley's manhood, was his great "lyrical drama," that splendid vision of the ultimate emancipation of humanity, the third and crowning part of the trinity of poems which show how the world may be regenerated by the power of love. The sonorous rhetoric of *Queen Mab* and the polemic narrative of *Laon and Cythna* were now succeeded and perfected by the solemn phantasies of *Prometheus Unbound*.

There is a legend told of one of Shelley's ancestors which may perhaps be considered as allegorical and prefigurative of this great humanitarian trilogy :—

> Sir Guyon de Shelley, one of the most famous of the Paladins, carried about with him at all times three conchs, fastened to the inside of his shield, tipt respectively with brass, with silver, and with gold. When he blew the first shell, all giants, however huge, fled before him. When he put the second to his lips, all spells were broken, all enchantments dissolved ; and when he made the third conch, the golden one, vocal, the law of God was immediately exalted, and the law of the devil annulled and abrogated wherever the potent sound reached.[1]

[1] Hogg's *Life of Shelley*.

Was Shelley thinking of this golden conch when he described, in his great poem, that "mystic shell" from which is sounded the trumpet-blast of universal freedom? For truly such a trumpet-blast, to those who have ears to hear and hearts to understand it, may be said to ring through every passage of *Prometheus Unbound*.

It was in the autumn of this same year, after the completion of his poetical masterpiece, that Shelley once more reverted to those social subjects of which he had treated in his Marlow pamphlets, and deserted, to quote his own words, "the odorous gardens of literature, to journey across the great sandy desert of politics." The time was an anxious and critical one, the bitter class-strife under which England had long been suffering having culminated on August 16 in the famous "Peterloo" massacre, when the soldiers fired on the unarmed people at a reform meeting near Manchester—the darkest hour, perhaps, of all the dark and disgraceful period of the Regency. Shelley, who, in spite of his absence in Italy, continued to take a deep interest in English politics, now conceived the notion of writing a series of political poems; but, though some of these were written and even forwarded to Leigh Hunt, they were not published till many years afterwards; while his *Philosophical View of Reform*, a prose essay written about the same time, is to this day hardly known except in excerpts and paraphrases.

In these writings Shelley never fails to enforce what he regarded as the central fact of the situation—that it is social, and not only political, reform that is needed to avert a revolution; wealth on the one hand and want on the other being the two fertile causes of discord and misery. In *The Mask of Anarchy*—that "flaming robe of verse," as Leigh Hunt called it—he asserted that real liberty cannot exist in a country where there is penury and starvation; while in the stirring lines, *To the Men of England*, we find the true democratic doctrine thus admirably and tersely expressed:—

> The seed ye sow another reaps;
> The wealth ye find another keeps;
> The robes ye weave another wears;
> The arms ye forge another bears.
>
> Sow seed—but let no tyrant reap;
> Find wealth—let no impostor heap;
> Weave robes—let not the idle wear;
> Forge arms—in your defence to bear.

But this defence was to be, according to Shelley's teaching, as far as possible a passive and constitutional protest. He had imbibed Godwin's strong abhorrence of any violent outbreak, and believed that it would be better and wiser to postpone even the attainment of reforms which are otherwise desirable, such as universal suffrage and the abolition of aristocracy, than to risk the stability of a righteous cause by any immature attempt at establishing a republic. It was because he aimed at a complete but bloodless revolution that he distrusted much of the teaching of Cobbett and his followers, in whose speeches he detected too many traces of the spirit of revenge.

On the other hand, he did not disguise his belief that if the aristocracy and plutocracy set themselves stubbornly against the gradual introduction of reforms, a forcible remedy would become justifiable. "I imagine," he says, "that before the English nation shall arrive at that point of moral and political degradation now occupied by the Chinese, it will be necessary to appeal to an exertion of physical strength."

During the latter half of 1819, the year in which these various works were produced, Shelley and Mary, having left Rome after the death of their child, were living at Leghorn and Florence, with Claire Clairmont still in their company. At Florence another son was born, on November 12, and was named Percy Florence. This event did much to raise the drooping spirits of the parents, and as it was felt that a more settled mode of life was now desirable, both for the infant's sake and for Shelley's health, which was affected by periodical attacks of spasms, the exact cause of which was never satisfactorily determined, they decided to take up their abode at Pisa, that place being especially recommended on account of the purity of the water. They accordingly left Florence early in the new year, and journeyed down the river Arno by boat.

Pisa soon became to Shelley in Italy what Marlow had been to him in England. He came there out of health and out of spirits, depressed by the apparent failure of his literary hopes, and disgusted by the coldness or insolence of the Englishmen he met abroad. Hitherto he and Mary had been leading a solitary and cheerless life among people with whom they were wholly out of sympathy; being, as Shelley had himself described it, "like a family of Wahabee Arabs, pitching their tent in the midst of London"; but at Pisa they found health and repose, and gradually gathered round them a circle of congenial and sympathetic friends. They stayed there during the whole of 1820 and 1821, with the exception of visits occasionally made to Leghorn, and more frequently to the baths of San Giuliano, a village distant about four miles; so that there was truth in Shelley's words when he wrote on a later occasion to Mary, "Our roots never struck so deeply as at Pisa, and the transplanted tree flourishes not."

The manner of Shelley's life at Pisa was much the

same as at Marlow. He was up early, and was busily engaged in reading or writing till two o'clock, with a hunch of dry bread beside him for food, and water for drink. Among his favourite books were Plato, the Greek dramatists, the Bible, Dante, Petrarch, Calderon, Goethe, Schiller, Shakespeare, Lord Bacon, Spinoza, and Milton. In the afternoon he would sail in his skiff on the Arno, or go off, book in hand, to the solitary pine-forests by the shore. In the evening he would again read, or devote the time to conversing with friends. Next to his books and his boat, Shelley's chief source of delight was in the numerous plants which he and Mary gathered round them in their Pisan home, and which throve well in that mild and equable climate; hence, perhaps, originated the idea of *The Sensitive Plant*, which was written at this date, and of *The Zucca*, written at Pisa in January, 1822. In a letter of the same month Shelley wrote: "Our windows are full of plants which turn the sunny winter into spring."

To society, in the conventional sense of the word, he was still as averse as ever, finding "saloons and compliments" too great bores to be endurable, and having the same horror as at Marlow of the wearisome visits of "idle ladies and gentlemen." "The few people we see," so he informed Medwin, "are those who suit us—and, I believe, nobody but us." He was also equally disinclined to dress in the approved fashion of society, declaring a hat to be little better than "a crown of thorns," and a stiff collar a halter. "I bear what I can, and suffer what I must," he groaned on one occasion, when compliance was demanded of him; but the Ariel in his nature could not often be induced thus to shackle itself in the prison-house of decorous costume.

At the beginning of their residence at Pisa the only

families with which the Shelleys were intimate were the
Gisbornes, who had a house at Leghorn, and the Tighes,
who lived at Pisa under the assumed name of Mr. and
Mrs. Mason; in both of which households Shelley found
enlightened views and opinions to a great extent in
accordance with his own. Maria Gisborne, once the
intimate friend of Godwin and Mary Wollstonecraft,
was a woman of quick intelligence and keen sensibility,
in whose society and conversation Shelley took much
pleasure, and by whom he was first introduced to the
study of the Spanish language, and especially the works
of Calderon. Mrs. Mason was a still more remarkable
character. As a girl she had been the pupil of Mary
Wollstonecraft, and had then become the wife of Lord
Mountcashel, from whom she was afterwards separated;
she was famous also as an ardent democrat, although a
countess, and a thoroughly patriotic Irishwoman, until
all her hopes were dashed by the disastrous Act of Union
in 1800. No wonder that Shelley and Mary spent much
time at the Masons' house at Pisa, and that they valued
the society of such friends, with whom they could freely
exchange opinions without being looked on with mistrust.
The correspondence with the Gisbornes was also a pleasure
to Shelley, and he took great interest in a scheme originated
by Henry Reveley, Mrs. Gisborne's son by a former marriage, for starting a steamer to ply between Leghorn and
Marseilles.

In the autumn of 1820 Claire Clairmont ceased to be a
regular inmate of Shelley's family, her misunderstandings
with Mary having rendered a change advisable. Sisters
by connection and not by birth, and differing widely in
character, Mary and Claire were not likely to be drawn
so closely together as to make it possible that they should
always have the same home. Claire was excitable, quick-

tempered, and prone to take offence on slight provocation ; and this accorded ill with Mary's calm, sedate, and somewhat exacting habit of mind. It was agreed, therefore, that Claire should take the post of governess in a family at Florence. Shelley, who was better able than Mary to sympathise with Claire, and was full of pity for her on account of the harsh treatment she received from Byron, and the prolonged separation from her child Allegra, did all he could to cheer and comfort her in her new position. Friendly correspondence was also maintained with Mary, and it was not long before Claire again visited them at Pisa.

The relations between Shelley and Claire Clairmont have been referred to by Matthew Arnold and other traducers of Shelley as an instance of his "inflammability." We are told by Dr. Dowden that some of Shelley's letters to Claire, "written when the sense of her desolate position was keen with him, contain utterances which, if we did not know how ardently Shelley gave himself away in friendship, might be regarded as the speech of a lover." This, however, is just what we *do* know of Shelley, for the knowledge is amply supplied in the reminiscences of his friends. He was emotional, warm-hearted, sympathetic, and in his relations with women, as with men, he disregarded conventional usages ; but at the same time his nature was so obviously free from any taint of grossness that words and actions which would have seemed suspicious in other men were felt by those who knew him to be, in his case, simple and harmless. This is placed beyond all doubt by the testimony of Hogg, who, cynic that he was, would have been the last man to be deceived by any fallacious plea of " platonic friendship." " It has happened," says Hogg, " that he had only one female disciple during the watches of the night, and the winged hours sped not less rapidly in interesting, engrossing debate. In two or three cases I have heard there was a noise about it, but most assuredly without other foundation than that such nocturnal consultations are unusual." [1]

We have seen how, in the preceding year, Shelley's interest had been aroused by the condition of the English working classes ; it was now to be arrested by the movements in favour of national independence, by which the South of Europe was agitated in 1820 and 1821. Spain was in arms against the tyranny of Ferdinand VII.; there was an insurrection at Naples against the dynasty of the Bourbons ; and Greece was already on the point of proclaiming its independence of Turkish misrule. Shelley, the consistent enemy of oppression in all its forms, was deeply interested in the cause of these rising nationalities, and it was his good fortune at this time to number among his friends some sincere and earnest-minded patriots. Vaccá, his medical adviser at Pisa, was not only a skilful and eminent physician, but an enthusiastic advocate of Italian freedom, and his professional visits to his friend and patient were the more helpful and beneficial alike to body and mind, since he wisely forebore to afflict Shelley with drugs, but was always ready to engage in a "profound and atheistical" conversation. Still more stimulating to Shelley's zeal was his friendship with Mavrocordato, the exiled Greek prince who afterwards became a leader in the Hellenic revolution, and who even now, inspired

---

[1] Trelawny's authority is to the same effect. He told Mr. W. M. Rossetti ("Talks with Trelawny," *Athenæum*, 1882) that Mary Shelley's "conjugal jealousy" was "baseless." The subject recalls to mind Shelley's own remark about the misunderstandings of his *Epipsychidion* : "I desired Ollier not to circulate this piece except to the συνετοί ; and even they, it seems, are inclined to approximate me to the circle of a servant-girl and her sweetheart."

by Shelley's prophetic spirit, was plotting revolt and looking forward to the emancipation of his fellow country-men.

It was at this time, and in these circumstances, that Shelley wrote his splendid odes *To Liberty* and *To Naples*, which were followed in 1821 by the still loftier and more ambitious *Hellas*, a poetic vision of the delivery of Greece, which was to a great extent realised by the result of the war of independence.

It is here worthy of note that Shelley's hatred of tyranny was not of that partial kind which sympathises warmly with the national aspirations of foreign countries, while remaining cold to equally important and equally justifiable movements at home. "There is no such thing as a rebellion in Ireland," he wrote in 1821, "nor anything that looks like it. The people are indeed stung to madness by the oppression of the Irish system, and there is no such thing as getting rents or taxes, even at the point of the bayonet, throughout the southern provinces. But there are no regular bodies of men in opposition to the Government, nor have the people any leaders." If the Irish people had then found leaders, as they have since done, there can be little question as to the bestowal of Shelley's sympathies.

At Pisa he was visited by his cousin and schoolfellow, Medwin, whom he had not seen for at least seven years. Since that time Medwin had become a cavalry officer, and had travelled in the East; but he still retained his habit of dabbling in poetry, and was soon as eager as ever to resume his joint literary labours with the fellow poet who had assisted him, nine years before, in such juvenile productions as *The Wandering Jew*. In spite of the carelessness and inaccuracy of which he was afterwards guilty as a biographer, Tom Medwin deserves to be kindly remembered by students of Shelley's life. Though vain and self-complacent by nature, he was sincerely impressed by the greatness of Shelley's genius, which in many ways he was better able to understand than were Hogg and Peacock, since he was at least free from the cynicism which made them blind to much that far less clever men could perceive and appreciate.

Among other acquaintances who occasionally figured in Shelley's circle were Sgricci, the famous Italian *improvisatore*, whose utterances in the theatre at Pisa greatly surprised and delighted Shelley; Count Taaffe, an eccentric Irishman, whose poetical pretensions caused much amusement to his audience; and Pacchiani, a disreputable professor, who made himself useful to the Shelleys by introducing them to more worthy friends— among them to Emilia Viviani, a name immortalised by the rapturous verses of the *Epipsychidion*.

It was a strange and memorable meeting in the Pisan convent of St. Anne between the beautiful and passionate-souled Italian girl, whose life was wasting away under the constraint of her enforced seclusion, and the young English poet, himself not unacquainted with tyranny and misfortune, who had devoted his whole being to the quest after that ideal beauty which, if it could be embodied in any earthly shape, might most surely be sought in the form of womanly perfection. It seemed to Shelley that in Emilia Viviani he had discovered a visible image and personification of the divine spirit of love, that "dim object of his soul's idolatry," which he had long worshipped by intuition, and to which he had always appealed as the one redeeming power by which a sorrowful world might be regenerated. From this spiritualised union of hearts sprang the rhapsody of the *Epipsychidion*, a poem ever sacred to the "esoteric few" for whom it was written, while, as Shelley remarked in his preface, "to a certain other class it must ever remain incomprehensible."

Years later, when Emilia had broken the bonds of an unhappy marriage—the still worse slavery for which she had been compelled to exchange her convent life— Medwin saw her at Florence shortly before her death. "I might fill many a page," he says, "by speaking of the tears she shed over the memory of Shelley."

Towards the end of 1821, after a pleasant summer spent chiefly at the baths of San Giuliano, where they had a boat on the canal that united the streams of the Arno and the Serchio, the Shelleys once more found themselves settled at Pisa, again surrounded by a considerable circle of friends. Claire, it is true, was no longer of their party; and Prince Mavrocordato had already sailed for Greece, to take part in the war of independence which was even now commencing; but the Masons were still living at Pisa, and Medwin returned there towards the close of the year. More important actors had also begun to appear on the scene.

Byron, to whom Shelley had paid a visit at Ravenna in August, had now transferred his household to Pisa for the winter months, and the friendly intercourse between the two poets was continued, until a coldness sprang up between them owing to the indignation felt by Shelley at Byron's conduct to Claire, whose daughter Allegra had been left, against the mother's wishes, in a convent near Ravenna. In the meantime a scheme had been started for the establishment of a new liberal periodical, to which Byron, Shelley, and Leigh Hunt should be the joint contributors; and in order to carry out this idea it was arranged that Leigh Hunt should shortly set out with his family and take up his abode at Pisa.

Vague hopes also floated through Shelley's mind of forming a larger colony of select spirits in his Italian home; he would be like Lucifer, and "seduce a third part of the starry flock." "I wish you, and Hogg and Hunt," so he had written to Peacock in the preceding year, "and I know not who besides, would come and spend some months with me together in this wonderful land." These wishes, however, were not fated to be realised. Peacock, who was now married, showed no inclination to leave his native country; and though a visit from Hogg was talked of, it was never carried out; while Horace Smith, a true friend, for whom Shelley always had a deep regard, was compelled to give up his intended journey on account of his wife's health; and Keats, another old acquaintance whom Shelley had hoped to see at Pisa, had died at Rome early in 1821, a loss commemorated by Shelley in the splendid elegy of the *Adonais*.

But, as a set-off against these losses and disappointments, Shelley and Mary had lately formed the closest and most intimate friendship of their married life—a friendship which was of special value to Shelley as affording him solace in his fits of dejection, and stimulating that passion for lyric composition to which his mind was now chiefly directed. It was by Medwin that the long-promised introduction was given; but when Shelley, writing in 1820, before Medwin's visit to Pisa, had expressed the hope of seeing "the lovely lady" and her husband on their arrival in Italy, and the conviction that such society would be of more benefit to his health than any medical treatment, he little thought how amply his words would be fulfilled. Who could have foreseen that the outcast poet, in his distant place of sojourn, would find a devoted friend and admirer in a

retired lieutenant of dragoons, who sixteen years before
this time had been his schoolfellow at Eton ; and, further,
that the wife of this friend would be discovered by Shelley
to be the "exact anti-type" of the guardian spirit of his
own "Sensitive Plant":—

> A lady, the wonder of her kind,
> Whose form was upborne by a lovely mind.

Yet so in reality it turned out; for none of Shelley's
friends—Leigh Hunt alone excepted—proved to be so
true and sympathetic as Edward Williams ; while Jane,
with her sweet voice and gentle manner, soon became to
the Pisan company, and to Shelley in particular, "a sort
of embodied peace in the midst of their circle of tempests."[1]
The Williamses had spent the summer of 1821 in a village
in the neighbourhood of San Giuliano, where Williams
and Shelley had been constantly together on the waters
of the Serchio Canal; and they were now living in the
same house with the Shelleys at Pisa, opposite the
mansion occupied by Byron on the Lung Arno.

Thither came also, before the winter was far advanced,
the latest but not least memorable of Shelley's friends, a
man "of savage but noble nature"—the dark, handsome
Trelawny, whose contempt for orthodox habits, together
with the adventurous seafarings of his early manhood,
seemed to indicate a mixture in his nature of pagan and
pirate. Like all who were brought into close connection
with Shelley, he soon became conscious of the indefinable
charm of the poet's character.

[1] "No sympathetic student of the poet's character and story," says
Mr. Cordy Jeaffreson, who will not be accused of an idolatrous partiality
for Shelley, "can entertain even a momentary suspicion of the refinement
and purity of Shelley's regard for the gentle and fine-natured woman to
whom he addressed the saddest and sweetest poetry of his life's closing
term. To say this of the feelings that swayed his soul in all its successive
services of homage towards his friend's wife is, indeed, to say no more than
I will declare of each and all of the so-called platonic attachments that
preceded the worship of Jane Williams."

Amid this congenial companionship Shelley was at the height of his powers. After devoting a long morning to that love of study which even the least literary of his friends found to be infectious in his company, he would be off with Edward Williams to breast the current of the Arno in his light skiff, his passion for boating still remaining as strong as ever ; or he would join Byron's party in riding or pistol-practice, his skill in the latter pastime giving proof that the imaginative temperament is not incompatible with a steady eye and hand; or he would walk abroad with Trelawny and other companions, all of whom he could distance by his long stride across broken ground. But his favourite haunts were the solitary sandy flats and the wild pine-forests that bordered the coast near the estuary of the Arno, where, as in the Bisham woods at Marlow, he could sit and write in complete quietude and seclusion, with no fear of human interruption to the visions that passed before him.

Here were written some of the most beautiful poems in that well-known series of lyrics addressed to Jane Williams, which was the chief production of Shelley's genius in the winter of 1821–1822. These lyrics, in the directness and simplicity of their style and the predominance of the personal element, reflect faithfully the feelings and workings of the mind of the revolutionary poet, when, after giving expression to the doctrines which he believed to be of vital importance to the welfare of mankind, and reaping the consequent harvest of hatred and misrepresentation, he paused awhile in his "passion for reforming the world," and solaced himself with the sympathy and friendship accorded him in all frankness and sincerity by a gentle and tender-hearted woman.

CHAPTER VIII.

COR CORDIUM

BEFORE the commencement of the hot weather in 1822, Shelley and Mary had moved their household from Pisa to the neighbourhood of Lerici, a small town on the Gulf of Spezzia, where they purposed spending the summer months. Edward and Jane Williams were again of the party, and Claire Clairmont, saddened now and subdued by the recent death of Allegra, was a visitor from time to time; but Trelawny still remained at Pisa in the company of Byron, with whom Shelley now held but little communication.

The Casa Magni, the house occupied by the Shelleys and Williamses, was a solitary and desolate-looking building, standing amid the wildest scenery of the Gulf of Spezzia, with a precipitous wooded slope behind it, and the sea in front. So close was it to the shore that the plash and moan of the waves could be heard in all the rooms, so that the inmates almost fancied themselves to be on board a ship in mid-sea, rather than lodged in a durable dwelling. At the very door of the house, or even within the large, unpaved entrance-hall, was kept the light skiff, made of canvas and reeds, in which Shelley, fond as ever of the paper boats of his boyhood, delighted to float on the waters of the bay, to the no slight alarm of his friends and neighbours. In addition to this fragile toy-boat, he was now the possessor of a small, undecked yacht, the *Ariel*, lately built for him at Genoa, in which he and Edward Williams could sail to Leghorn and other neighbouring ports, and meditated still longer voyages along the Mediterranean coasts.

It was a pleasant change to Shelley, this relapse into wild, unconventional life, after the comparatively large demands made on his time by his acquaintances at Pisa; and he was never happier than when sailing in his *Ariel* under the blazing Italian sun, or listening to the music of Jane's guitar on the moonlit terrace of the Casa Magni. He was in no mood at this time for any great creative work, or for any close co-operation in the joint literary enterprise for which Leigh Hunt was already on his way to meet Byron at Pisa. To Mary, who was in weak health when they came to Lerici, there was something ominous and disquieting in the "unearthly beauty" of the place, and the savage wildness of its scenery; but Shelley only felt the influence of these surroundings in a sense of passiveness and suspension. "I stand, as it were, upon a precipice," so he wrote in June, "which I have ascended with great, and cannot descend without greater, peril; and I am content if the heaven above me is calm for the passing moment."

For the moment the heaven was calm, but the calmness was of that kind which too often precedes and prognosticates a storm. The droughts of the early summer were followed by a period of fierce heat and sultry splendour; day after day the sun blazed down with unabated fury on sea and land, while prayers were offered up in churches for the rain that was still withheld. There was something expectant and portentous in the season, and this perhaps awoke a similar feeling in the minds of the two families at the Casa Magni. Shelley himself, though he did not share Mary's vague apprehensions and distrust of Lerici and its wild neighbourhood, was haunted by strange visions which surprised those to whom he told them at the time, and were afterwards remembered. On one occasion it was the face of his former child-friend, Allegra, that looked forth and smiled on him from the waves; on another it was his own wraith that met him, cloaked and hooded, on the terrace of the house; on a third it was the figure of Edward Williams, pale and dying, that appeared to him in a dream, with the tidings that the sea was even then flooding the house in which they were sleeping. Nor was it only the vivid imagination of the poet that was thus disturbed, for Jane Williams was also troubled with the apparition of what she took to be Shelley, at times when Shelley himself was far absent and out of sight; and, in addition to these mysterious day-dreams and midnight panics, there was always present to the minds of Shelley's friends the real fear that his life might some day be sacrificed to the element which he loved so well, but which had so often threatened to engulf him.

But still the heaven remained calm, and still Shelley was happy while he basked in the full heat of the Italian summer, writing his poem on *The Triumph of Life* as he cruised in his yacht along the picturesque windings of the coast, or drifted in the little skiff across the land-locked waters of the bay. In *The Triumph of Life*, which caught its tone and colour as much from the scenery and season in which it was written as from the transient mood of its author, we have a mystical description of the pomp and pageantry of that triumphal procession in which the spirit of Man is dragged captive behind the chariot of Life. It is no recantation of idealism—as some readers, misled by the despondent spirit of the poem, have been too quick to assume—but rather, like *Alastor*, a recognition of the price that even the greatest idealists must pay to reality; it is the cost, not the failure, of the ideal philosophy that is here allegorically represented; and it is probable that if the poem, which was left a fragment, had been completed by Shelley, it would have dealt with the saving influence and regenerating power of Love.

It is not credible that Shelley could have given up his ideal faith without his friends noticing and recording so momentous a change—indeed, the evidence of his biographers, so far as it goes, points to exactly the opposite conclusion. Speaking of his writings of the previous autumn, Mary Shelley afterwards recorded that his opinions then remained unchanged. "By those opinions," she said, "carried even to their utmost extent, he wished to live and die, as being in his conviction not only true, but such as alone would conduce to the moral improvement and happiness of mankind."

But though Shelley's faith in love and liberty was unshaken, he had learnt by long and bitter experience that it can only be upheld at the cost of much personal error and painful collision with the established system of society. Now, as at previous periods of his life, the ill-will and hostility of his calumniators had wrought a temporary discouragement, a disposition to look on the darker rather than the brighter aspect of his fortunes, to contemplate the loss incurred rather than the success achieved.

Can it be wondered that so sensitive a nature as Shelley's should at times have shrunk instinctively from further contact with this world of men by whom he seemed destined to be for ever misunderstood, even as their motives were to him unintelligible? Some months before the time of which I speak his eager fancy had pictured the relief of retiring with those he loved to some solitary island—a Greek island, perhaps, and part of a free Hellas redeemed from the Turkish oppressor—and there dwelling in blissful seclusion, far from the miserable jealousies and contagion of the world. Then the dream had taken the still stranger form of a desire to obtain political employment at the court of some Indian potentate, such as those of whom he had heard Williams and Medwin discourse; he would be an Avatar, and dispense his blessings in the far regions of the East, instead of casting his poems before the cold, ungrateful West, as "jingling food for the hunger of oblivion." And now, at Lerici, when the balance of the season and of his own destiny seemed to be hanging in suspense, the thought even of suicide was not wholly absent from his mind as a dim possibility of the future; at any rate, it comforted him to feel that he might possess this "golden key to the chamber of perpetual rest."

Yet it must not be supposed that this despondent mood had made Shelley morbid in his habits or less helpful and kindly to those around him; on the contrary, he impressed those who saw him at this time with the belief that he was now physically and intellectually as strong and healthy as at any other period of his life; and the visits and assistance which he rendered to his poverty-stricken neighbours in the cottages near the Casa Magni, as at Marlow, were long gratefully remembered. The gentleness and benevolence of this supposed enemy of mankind were still written very legibly in his features.[1] "If he is not pure and good," said a lady who had met him at Pisa, "then there is no truth and goodness in this world"; and even a hostile reviewer in a London periodical was fain to admit that it was

1 "THERE was the very Best of men, and he was treated as the very Worst," said Trelawny to Swinburne, more than fifty years later.

"not in his outer semblance, but in his inner man, that the explicit demon was seen." To his intimate friends no traces of this "explicit demon" were discoverable; but they did feel that there was something in Shelley's nature too subtle and spiritual to be gauged by the ordinary estimate of humanity; and their feelings found expression in such nicknames as "Ariel" and "The Snake," as he came and went like a spirit, with glittering eyes and noiseless step, an enigma and a mystery even to those who were nearest to him and most dear.

And, indeed, very impressive was the figure of this young man of twenty-nine, who was commonly regarded by those who knew him only through hearsay as a monster of wickedness, while those immediately around him were convinced that he was the gentlest and least selfish of men. His bent and emaciated form, his features which betrayed signs of acute mental suffering, and his hair already interspersed with grey, gave him at times the appearance of premature age; yet the spirit of triumphant energy and indomitable youth which had sustained him, and still sustained him, through all his misfortunes, was never wholly absent from his countenance and demeanour. He was still the unwearied student, the eager controversialist, and the enthusiastic votary of freedom; yet he was subject now perhaps more than in his earlier years to moods of despondency which his friends regarded as "a melancholy too sacred to notice." [1]

Nor was it surprising that he was thus affected; for he had "run the gauntlet," to quote his own words,

---

[1] The following is the description given by the artist William E. West, who met Shelley at Lord Byron's: "Never have I seen a face so expressive of ineffable goodness. Its benignity and intelligence were only shadowed by a certain sadness, as of one upon whom life pressed keenly, at touching variance with the youth indicated by his contour and movements."

"through a hellish society of men." The religious, ethical, and political speculations which he had advanced in *Queen Mab*, *Laon and Cythna*, *Prometheus Unbound*, and his other writings, had brought down on him a foul storm of obloquy and misrepresentation; he who above all men was filled with love, reverence, and natural piety, was branded as a desperate atheist and wanton blasphemer; while the most wild and ludicrous calumnies respecting the conduct of his life were freely circulated and credited.

In 1819 the *Quarterly Review* had published a criticism of *Laon and Cythna*, and the writer had not scrupled to lend himself to the basest and most reckless insinuations on Shelley's private character, assuming the tone of one who was behind the scenes on subjects of which it is now evident that he was ignorant.

> "If we might withdraw the veil of private life," wrote this pious moralist, "and tell what we *now* know about him, it would be indeed a disgusting picture that we should exhibit, but it would be an unanswerable comment on our text; it is not easy for those who read only to conceive how much low pride, how much cold selfishness, how much unmanly cruelty are consistent with the laws of this universal and lawless love."

Ridiculous as such assertions as this were seen to be when the true outlines of Shelley's life were published, they constituted at the time a very grave annoyance and even danger, for they were widely disseminated and almost universally believed. It is said that Shelley, during his residence in England, contemplated the possibility of being some day condemned to the public pillory; and who can say that in that age of tyrannical prosecutions such a fear was altogether groundless? In Italy he more than once met with rudeness, or even violent insult, at the hands of his fellow countrymen, whose minds were vehemently prejudiced against him by the reports published in the press. "The calumnies, the sources of which are probably deeper than we perceive, have ultimately for object the depriving us of the means of security and subsistence." So Shelley wrote to Mary from Ravenna in 1821, with reference to the slander of which he and Claire were the victims.

In the meantime no calmness of sky or sea could allay Mary Shelley's unaccountable but persistent anxiety. "During the whole of our stay at Lerici," so she afterwards wrote, "an intense presentiment of coming evil brooded over my mind, and covered this beautiful place and genial summer with the shadow of coming misery." Constitutionally prone to fits of dejection, she had meditated long before on the solemn and pathetic subject of the flight of time, how swiftly the future becomes the present, and the present the past, and how in the last moment of life all is found to be but a dream. Her life with Shelley had now extended over almost eight years— years full of strange vicissitudes and mingled happiness and sorrow, but cheered throughout by the sense of the mutual love and respect that existed between them.

For in spite of their natural dissimilarity in character, as shown in Mary's occasional coldness, and her greater regard for conventionalities and the opinion of society— "that mythical monster, Everybody," as Shelley called it—their union had been a true one. What if this bond, that had survived the shock and strain of so many troubles and calamities, were now about to be severed ?

Such was the dim, unformed thought that darkened Mary's mind when, on July 1, Shelley left Lerici in company with Edward Williams, and sailed in the *Ariel* to Leghorn in order to greet Leigh Hunt, who had now arrived in Italy.

Very cordial and affectionate was the meeting between the two friends, who had not seen each other for more than four years and had much to talk over and communicate. The next few days were spent by Shelley at Pisa, and were devoted chiefly to arranging Leigh Hunt's affairs and negotiating with Byron on his friend's behalf respecting the forthcoming periodical. On the following Sunday, these affairs being settled, Shelley and Leigh Hunt visited the chief buildings of Pisa, among them the cathedral, where, as they listened to the rolling tones of the organ, Shelley warmly assented to Leigh Hunt's remark that the world might yet see a divine religion, of which the principle would be sought not in faith, but in love. The same evening he bid farewell to the Hunts, Mrs. Mason, and other friends in Pisa, and returned to Leghorn, in order to sail homewards with Edward Williams on the following day.

It was the early afternoon of Monday, July 8, when the *Ariel* sailed out of Leghorn harbour, on its computed journey of seven or eight hours. On the same afternoon the long tension of the oppressive summer weather was relaxed; the sultry spell was at last broken; and the dull, ominous calm of the preceding weeks found voice and spoke its secret in a single burst of sudden and irresistible storm. That night the thunder played loudly along the Italian coast, and the din of winds and waves and rain carried doubt and terror to several anxious English hearts. In the lonely house by the Gulf of Spezzia two women were eagerly expecting their husbands' return; at Pisa, Mrs. Mason dreamed that Shelley was dead, and awoke weeping bitterly; while, at Leghorn, Trelawny was awaiting the dawn with grave anxiety, for the last that had been seen of Shelley's boat was its entry into the dense sea-fog that preceded the rushing tempest.

> The massy earth and spherèd skies are riven !
> I am borne darkly, fearfully, afar.

So Shelley had written, as if by some prophetic instinct, in the concluding stanza of his *Adonais ;* and who shall say that so swift and mysterious a death was not the fittest ending to a life so full of wonder and mystery ? His task on earth was now accomplished ; his message of love was delivered ; and the pure spirit, purged of the last dross of mortality, was summoned

> Back to the burning fountain whence it came.

After ten days of cruel suspense, two bodies were cast up by the sea on the coast between Pisa and Spezzia, and were identified as those of Shelley and Williams. The Italian quarantine laws for the prevention of plague being most strictly enforced, the bodies were at once buried in the sands—in those very sands over which Shelley had but lately ridden in company with Byron and other friends—until arrangements had been made with the authorities at Florence for their disinterment and cremation. This ceremony took place on August 15 and 16, the body of Williams being burned on the former day, and that of Shelley on the latter, in the presence of numerous spectators, among whom were Byron, Trelawny, and Leigh Hunt.

It was a scene that impressed itself ineffaceably on the memory of those who witnessed it—the vast expanse of yellow sand, unbroken by sign of human dwelling; the blue and cloudless sky; the sea calm and smiling; the distant outline of marble-crested Apennines; and in the centre of the group of bystanders the fierce flame that rose from the funeral-pile, quivering with extraordinary clearness from the frankincense, oil, and wine that were plentifully poured over it ; while close above, in the tremulous and glassy atmosphere, a solitary curlew wheeled and circled with strange pertinacity. "One might have expected," said Leigh Hunt, "a sun-bright countenance to look out of the flame, coming once more before it departed, to thank the friends who had done their duty." There was, indeed, something in the nature of the wild scene and the pagan ceremony that was appropriate to the obsequies of one who was himself a Greek in his instinctive reverence for the elemental purity of sea and fire.

It was Trelawny who had undertaken and who faithfully discharged the duty of conducting the search for the bodies of Shelley and Williams, and of carrying the news to the two widows. It was he, too, who at the end of the cremation snatched Shelley's heart, which remained unconsumed, from the flames, and collected the ashes in a coffer, in order that they might be buried at Rome in the same Protestant burying-place where Shelley's child had been laid, a spot which the poet had long before described as "the most beautiful and solemn cemetery" he ever beheld. To Leigh Hunt belongs the honour of having suggested the inscription on the tombstone of the words *Cor Cordium*—a perfect tribute of reverence and affection to the memory of that heart of hearts whose overmastering passion, the source of all its strength and all its weakness, had been the love of humankind.

Nor was it only Trelawny and Leigh Hunt who thus gave proof of their affection. A week after the burning of the bodies, the lonely house at Lerici, now unfurnished and deserted by its former inhabitants, was visited by a solitary traveller, who had turned out of his course, as he journeyed from Pisa to Genoa, to perform this last act of melancholy pilgrimage. It was "poor Tom Medwin," as Shelley had called him, who, poetaster though he was, could yet feel keenly the supreme sadness of gazing on those empty and silent rooms that had so lately been filled with the voices of life and happiness, and of standing on the seaward-facing terrace where Shelley had so often listened with delight to Jane Williams's simple melodies. As he passed through the rude entrance-hall on the ground floor, Medwin noticed oars and fragments of spars lying scattered in confusion, and among them the broken frame of Shelley's favourite skiff, destined never again to find so venturesome a pilot.

And where, meantime, was the *Ariel* herself? She was discovered by some sailors, employed by Trelawny for that purpose, sunk in ten or fifteen fathoms of water, about two miles off the coast, and, being raised in the following September, was found to have her gunwale stove in, as if she had been run down by an Italian felucca during the squall; whence arose the suspicion, which has never been satisfactorily proved or disproved, that there was an intent to plunder the vessel of some money which was known to be on board. Having been repaired and rigged afresh, the *Ariel* was again sent to sea; but she proved unseaworthy, and a second time suffered shipwreck. "Her shattered planks," wrote Mrs. Shelley in 1839, "now lie rotting on the shore of one of the Ionian islands on which she was wrecked." Strange that the *Ariel*'s existence should have ended on one of those very Greek islands to which Shelley's fancy had so often been attracted as a possible home and place of refuge from the calamities that beset him !

For a year after her husband's death, Mary Shelley

remained in Italy, unable to tear herself away from the land of their adoption, in spite of the many painful memories it awakened. In all the records of fact and fiction it would be difficult to find anything more pathetic than the published extracts from the journal she kept during those first dreary months of bereavement and solitude. The thought and image of Shelley were ever present to her mind—now it was the tone of Byron's voice that, by sheer force of old association, would make her listen for *that other* voice which, when Byron spoke, had ever been wont to reply; now, as she mused and read in a fit of deep abstraction, it was Shelley himself who seemed to call her, as a sudden voice cried "Mary!" The sense of utter loneliness was only relieved by the hopes of rejoining, in another existence, that swift and gentle soul who in his earthly incarnation had been like a caged spirit, "an elemental being, enshrined in a frail image." But this desire for death was not yet to be gratified; there was first a long course of widowhood to be encountered and lived through, her aged father to be cheered and tended, her child to be educated, and, most sacred charge of all, her husband's writings to be collected and given to the world.[1]

Meanwhile, in solid contrast to these shifting scenes of life and death, grief and pleasure, rapturous aspiration and heaviest dejection, Sir Timothy Shelley, now an old man of seventy years of age, still lived on, as stern and unyielding as ever. Nothing to him were the strangest events of that strange drama of a lifetime, that "miracle of thirty years," of which the secret and motive power were love; Field Place still remained as it had been

[1] It would be easy to dwell on the commonplaceness of Mary Shelley's life and character when disunited from Shelley's. I prefer not to do so. If she became "respectable" in her later years, let us remember that she had suffered what might have broken a far stronger spirit than hers.

when its doors were first closed against the youthful offender who, by his reprehensible thirst for knowledge, had incurred the anger of learned men entrusted with his education. Eleven years had now passed since Sir Timothy, writing to the father of Shelley's college friend and fellow-culprit, had insisted on the necessity of keeping " my young man and your young man " apart. And now this young man had run a desperate and erratic career, in which a few misguided people affected to see a subject for interest and approval, but which had brought down on him the unsparing condemnation of the Lord Chancellor, the *Quarterly Review*, and all that England possessed of wealth, religion, and respectability.

The dishonour to Field Place was deep and indelible; there was one thing, however, which was still within Sir Timothy's power, as it was clearly his duty, to contrive. He could take advantage of his control of the purse to forbid his son's widow writing a life of the poet, and thus further disgracing the Shelley family by the publication of deeds which it was far wiser to consign to a charitable forgetfulness. Moreover, that an innocent child might not suffer for the offences of guilty parents, Sir Timothy offered to undertake the maintenance of his infant grandson on condition that he was wholly taken from his mother's charge. This offer, it is needless to say, was refused by Mary Shelley. " Why, I live only to keep him from their hands," was the entry in her journal.

So Sir Timothy Shelley, by no means breathing reconciliation, lived on till he had completed his ninetieth year, a life three times the length of that of his unnatural son; and when he died, no " *Cor Cordium*," but a flattering description of the conventional kind, was set up to blazon his virtues on the

walls of Horsham Church. It may be, however, that
those who thoughtfully ponder the contrast between
these two lives, and the lessons conveyed by each, will
see in the contrast a striking instance of the truth of
an old poet's words :—

> Circles are praised, not that abound
> In largeness, but the exactly round ;
> So life we praise that does excel,
> Not in much time, but living well.

Shelley himself, as I have already said, must be
regarded as a representative of the future and nobler
social state, a prophet and forerunner of the higher
intellectual development, a soul sent on earth before
its due season by some strange freak, or rather, let us
say, by some benignant disposition of destiny. The
religion which he preached, with love for its faith, and
natural piety towards all living things for its command-
ment, has this supreme advantage over the creed of the
theologian, that it can look with confidence instead of
suspicion on the advance of science, and find a friend
instead of an enemy in time.

But this religion, being a religion of the future, is for
that very reason meaningless and unacceptable to those
who, by sentiment or circumstance, are upholders of the
present system—that is to say, the great bulk of society.
Many people are naturally incapable of sympathising
with Shelley's creed, perceiving in it nothing but a cold
and brilliant display of intellectual subtleties ; while
others are roused to positive hatred by his aggressive
attitude. All this is natural and inevitable enough ; for,
since the prophet is proverbially without honour among
the mass of his own generation, it was not to be expected
that the full significance of Shelley's career should be
appreciated by that very society whose displacement he

heralded. Shelley's good fame, both as regards the rightness of his personal conduct and the soundness of his views, can afford to wait till a new wave of evolution has swept away the present barriers of prejudice and intolerance.

In the meanwhile, he will not be unhonoured of the discerning few who, reading the signs of the time, can already perceive that the great social and ethical questions which are gradually being recognised as of primary importance to the welfare of the community are precisely those on which he instinctively fixed his attention. It is for this reason, and not only because he is our greatest lyric poet, that Shelley's life and doctrines are deserving of more general study than is at present accorded them; and those who love and admire him are not likely to be affected by the idle taunt, so often levelled at them by their opponents, that they are attributing an absurd "infallibility" to his opinions, and an absurd "perfection" to his character. Shelley, the votary of liberty and free thought, who in spite of his wide reading was so entirely devoid of the academic spirit, was the last person who would have wished to found a "school," or be regarded as a "master"; and the respect that is now felt for his writings is not based on any superstitious or sentimental reverence for the *ipse dixit* of the poet, but simply on the fact that his opinions are being more and more corroborated by experience and time.

In the same way, not even the most uncompromising admirers of Shelley's character need be suspected of the intent to endow him with an unnatural perfection, because they decline to subscribe to that modern fear of hero-worship which makes most of our critics, disbelieving in the existence of any truly heroic figure in this age of mediocrity, so careful to mete out praise and blame in nicely balanced portions, like a grocer dealing out his wares in a succession of sweets and acids. However justifiable our dread of mere sentimental eulogy, we may surely venture to speak generously and unreservedly in our praise of a man whose great primary qualities of unworldliness and sincerity drew unstinted tributes of admiration from those who knew him personally, even when they chanced to be cynical lawyers, satirical novelists, bluff sailors, retired cavalry officers, or misanthropic poets.

Such homage paid to such a character does not imply that we are blind to the many foibles, eccentricities, and minor blemishes by which even the noblest nature may be crossed and chequered, and from which Shelley was certainly not exempt. We are well aware that his life, except in its one dominant feature, was a strange mixture of contrary tendencies and varying moods. He was hopeful and despondent, strong and weak, graceful and awkward, frugal and lavish, serious and playful, wise and whimsical, forbearing and charitable to a singular degree in his intercourse with friend or foe, yet on rare occasions hasty and unjust in his judgments; by habit candid and trustworthy, yet sometimes led on by a predilection for mystery, and by an extreme dislike of causing pain or disappointment, to be evasive and circuitous in his dealings. But while he was thus, to some extent, the creature of conflicting moods and circumstances—" chased by the spirit of his destiny," as he himself expressed it, " from purpose to purpose, like clouds by the wind "—it is important to remember that these contradictions and weaknesses lay on the surface of his nature, and not at its core; for his character in all vital and essential points was strikingly firm and consistent, his innate and solid virtues standing him in good stead at all the great and fateful crises of his mature life.

Few lives have been subjected to such a searching scrutiny as that which Shelley's has undergone, and still fewer have come forth from the ordeal so unscathed. But, as I have insisted all along, his actions must, in common honesty, be interpreted by his own standard of morality, and not by that which it was his special object to discredit and overthrow. This is the only key to a right understanding of his career; and if this rational principle be adopted, it will be found to explain much that has hitherto seemed unaccountable. Difficulties there must always be in estimating so subtle and complex a character; but, whatever mystery may still hang over certain episodes, the general effect and leading purpose of Shelley's life will be seen to be singularly harmonious and clear.

CHAPTER IX.

THE POET

IT ought not to be forgotten, in view of the general acceptance of Shelley by present-day critics as a great master of song, that this conclusion, so far from being naturally and spontaneously arrived at, was forced on the literary profession by a long and bitter controversy. Seventy years ago it was the almost unanimous opinion of the most eminent and respected *littérateurs* that Shelley was a wretched poetaster of the most worthless kind.[1] The two fatal defects pointed out in his writings by the *Quarterly Review* (1821) were the want of music and the want of meaning—*i.e.*, the want of everything that goes to the making of genuine poetry.

"The rhythm of the verse is often harsh and unmusical" was the first complaint of the reviewer; and he proceeded to insist that "the predominating character of Mr. Shelley's poetry is its frequent and total want of meaning." Among instances adduced of this fault were "something that is done by a Cloud," reference being made to the last and most beautiful stanza of the lyric of that name; the "debut of the Spirit of the Earth," in Act III. of *Prometheus Unbound;* the comparison of a poet to a chameleon, which was shown to have "no

---

[1] There were, however, a few exceptions to this judgment. "The disappearance of Shelley from the world," wrote Beddoes in 1824, "seems, like the tropical setting of that luminary to which his poetical genius can alone be compared, with reference to the companions of his day, to have been followed by instant darkness and owl-season." Shelley's high poetical gift was freely recognised by Macaulay and a small but brilliant circle of Cambridge students. Moultrie's poem, *The Witch of the North*, 1824, contains passages which are direct imitations of Shelley's *Witch of Atlas*.

more meaning than the jingling of the bells on a fool's cap, and far less music"; and the stanza of the *Sensitive Plant* concerning "the hyacinth purple and white and blue," which was held up to special ridicule. "In short," said the reviewer, summing up the qualities of the most splendid volume of lyrics that Shelley ever published, "it is not too much to affirm that in the whole volume there is not one original image of nature, one simple expression of human feeling, or one new association of the appearances of the moral with those of the material world," the sole merit that could be allowed the poet being "considerable mental activity." In conclusion, this representative critic, chuckling at his own humour, quoted the final passage of Act III. of *Prometheus Unbound*, printing it like prose in continuous sentences, and then gaily informed his readers that it was meant by its author for verse, "since Mr. Shelley's poetry is, in sober sadness, drivelling prose run mad."

This is a fair sample of the sort of appreciation awarded to Shelley by contemporary reviewers.[1] But forty years later a great change had come over the critical verdict, and the *Quarterly Review* was affected by it. The lyrics of *Prometheus Unbound*, which in 1821 had less music than the bells of a fool's cap, were praised by the reviewer of 1861 as "moving and exquisite poetry," while the drama as a whole was spoken of as "a grand conception" and "a great work." Twenty-six years more, and the conversion of the *Quarterly* was complete. The reviewer of 1887 found he had no course open to him but to follow still further the path on which his forerunner had entered, and to entirely disavow the

---

[1] The *Literary Gazette*, September 9, 1820, was equally contemptuous, and described *Prometheus Unbound* as the "stupid trash of a delirious dreamer."

earlier critic who had sought to destroy Shelley's poetical
reputation. The "drivelling prose run mad" is now
transfigured into "the statuesque and radiant beauty"
of *Prometheus Unbound*, which drama is further described
as "a dizzy summit of lyric inspiration, where no foot
but Shelley's ever trod before." Even the *Cloud*, whose
metamorphoses so severely puzzled the wiseacre of 1821,
is declared to be inspired by "the essential spirit of
classic poets"; and we learn with a satisfaction enhanced
by the source of the confession that "there are but two
or three poets at the most whom literature could less
afford to lose than this solitary master of ethereal verse."
After such praise from such a quarter, the question of
Shelley's poetical genius may well be considered to be
at an end.

Truly in this case time has proved to be a signal
avenger, since less than a century has witnessed the
ignominious reversal of the most approved critical judgments. The *Quarterly Review* claimed to be able to
instruct the general public on points of literary taste ;
and we have seen that in its estimate of Shelley's poems
it has been compelled entirely to recast its earlier
opinions. The attempt now made to excuse the former
unjust depreciation of Shelley's literary genius, because
of his social heresies, is singularly feeble ; for though an
ordinary reader might be pardoned for not discovering
the poetical value of writings which for other reasons he
disliked, this could be no valid excuse for the blindness
of a professed reviewer, whose special duty it was to
separate the good from the bad. Yet we find the latest
Quarterly reviewer complacently remarking that "the
attitude in which Shelley stands towards the past, the
present, and the future explains the unreasoning neglect
of his poetic genius during his life."

True, it explains ; but it is very far from being a justification. On the contrary, it suggests the remark that the highest literary verdicts, on any new and original poetry, are almost invariably wrong. This may seem a hard saying, but facts show it to be a just one, nor is the reason far to seek. For as each age has its own ideal of what is " correct " in literature, so has it a body of cultured and accomplished critics—on their own lines, and within their own limits, the " best judges " of their generation—who apply the standard of the current ideal to every literary production. In a large number of instances—to wit, in every case where the subject of the criticism is an attempt to conform to the ideal of the day— the judgment may be a sound one; but the moment a great original writer appears on the scene, with new ideas, new faith, new art, and new manner of expression, the old standard of criticism becomes inapplicable. None the less it is so applied, with great confidence and dignity, by its accredited professors, and the result, though in fact a quite ludicrous fiasco, is respectfully received by the public.

Every literary period has its Pope or its Tennyson, a great master of some fashionable contemporary style, which is powerful enough to afford a model and standard for the critics to work with, but not so uncomfortably powerful as to raise the bogey of " social ideas," or to put any severe strain on the intellectual capacity of its worshippers. The Pope of Shelley's period was none other than Thomas Campbell, the best of good fellows and the pleasantest of second-rate poets, who, from the publication of *Gertrude of Wyoming* in 1809 to his death in 1844, was regarded in literary circles and by the general public as the greatest English poet of the nineteenth century, with the possible exception of Lord

Byron. "You did not do all this to Burns," wrote Campbell (who, to do him justice, was more aware of the absurdity of his position than some of our other Popes have been), "you neglected *him*, a real genius, a wonder; and you bestow all this on me, who am nothing, compared to him."

It was therefore perfectly inevitable, and in that sense perfectly satisfactory, that Shelley's poetical pretensions should be ridiculed by a generation which detested Wordsworth, and never discovered Blake; and, in so far as it recognised the greatness of Lord Byron, was attracted by his most superficial qualities rather than his most enduring ones—by his sentimentalism and egoism and misanthropy, rather than by his scathing hatred of hypocrisy and oppression. It was equally inevitable as years went on, and the new literary and social ideals began to assert themselves, that a new criterion of poetry should mould itself on those forms, and the old anti-Shelleyan verdicts should be gradually rescinded. All this, I say, is satisfactory enough; but when we hear some cultured professor of the present time enlarging on Shelley's proud position among the poets (and perhaps in the same breath denouncing his religious and social views as visionary or immoral), be it remembered that such partial acceptance of Shelley is based on no real insight or genuine appreciation, but is merely a testimony that a great poetical genius has triumphed over a hostile criticism, and that the very persons who, like their forefathers, would have condemned him, ninety years ago, as a meaningless poetaster, are now content to sing his praises as a great lyrical poet.

How deeply rooted is the dislike which the literary profession has at heart felt for Shelley, though now constrained by force of circumstances to yield him effusive lip-homage, is shown by the utterances of Matthew Arnold, a critic whose privileged position and dogmatic temper impelled him at times to give free vent to opinions which his faithful henchmen of the press have found to be a rather embarrassing legacy. For example, it has been surmised that, "when Arnold spoke as if Shelley's prose might survive his poetry, we may presume that this was merely his fun, though the humour be rather subterranean."[1] There is not, of course, the very slightest ground for such a presumption; for Arnold, in his refusal to accept Shelley as a great poet, was not only unmistakably in earnest, but was courageously reverting to a critical judgment which is far more in accord with the *real* sentiments of the cultured classes than the vapid eulogies of which Shelley is now the recipient. It is a fact that Arnold could see nothing in Shelley's poetry, and that Arnold was the reputed master-critic, the Superior Person *par excellence*, of modern English literature.

I have advisedly headed this chapter "The Poet," because I wish to guard myself against the absurd charge which is often brought against those who lay stress on the importance of the Shelleyan principles— that, in their zeal to represent the poet as a revolutionist, they are depreciating the imaginative element which is the true glory of his genius. It is amusing to find that the very persons who have blamed Shelley for "incoherence" are the first to resent an exposition of the clear message that runs through the whole body of his writings, on the plea that the ethereal sublimities of the lyrist would be wronged by any mundane association with the mere philosopher or politician! Now, of

---

[1] *Saturday Review*, September 14, 1889.

course, a genuine liking for lyric poetry is a gift that is innate in a man, and cannot be acquired by study—it is either there or not there from the beginning, and it is either there or not there to the end; so that there are doubtless many students of Shelley, among all classes of his readers, whether revolutionists or the contrary, who miss much of what is most subtle and impalpable in his verse. But I will assert that, where this lyrical sense is present, the man who understands Shelley as a pioneer will understand him the better, not the worse, as a poet. The reader who most fully sympathises with the ideas that underlie the polemical rhetoric of *Queen Mab* will also most fully sympathise with the soaring raptures of *Prometheus Unbound*.

No whole-hearted admirer of Shelley would ever question that it is as Poet that he holds the surest claim to immortality. His poetry was the supreme expression, the crowning flower, of a singularly beautiful life, and the unspeakable magic of his verse will doubtless outlast even the far fulfilment of the prophecies which that verse conveys. By none will this truth be more freely recognised than by those who are thorough believers in the essential rightness of his principles; for assuredly they love his poems with a love exceeding that of any intellectual creed. To them there has been a joy unfailing in each well-remembered cadence, in the lines that haunt the memory like the notes of aerial music, in the words that appear, as has been well said of them, "to throb with living lustres"; to them one single spirit-song from the tumultuous harmonies of his lyrical masterpiece is more precious than all the "systems" that the mind of democrat can devise.

> Life of Life! thy lips enkindle
>   With their love the breath between them;

And thy smiles before they dwindle
   Make the cold air fire ; then screen them
In those looks, where whoso gazes
Faints, entangled in their mazes.

Child of Light ! thy limbs are burning
   Thro' the vest which seems to hide them ;
As the radiant lines of morning
   Thro' the clouds ere they divide them ;
And this atmosphere divinest
Shrouds thee wheresoe'er thou shinest.

But though Shelley's spirituality was the highest element of his genius, let us not forget that it was but a part—if the most glorious part—of his whole mental condition. It is as impossible for a lofty imagination to be independent of a sound intellectual basis as for a rose-tree to have blossom without root ; and if Shelley's ideals had been the pernicious nonsense which contemporary moralists imagined, his poetry must perforce have been nonsensical also. Right thought, true feeling, must underlie the most ethereal structures of the fancy, though, of course, there need be no obtrusive expression of what can best be indirectly conveyed. The modern academic theory—sedulously fostered by men who, with regard to all the vital issues of the age, live in a fools' paradise of indifference—the theory that great literature must be kept "pure" of all association with ethics, is one which found no favour with Shelley. From his *Defence of Poetry* I take the following characteristic passage on the poetical function :—

> But poets, or those who imagine and express this indestruc-
> tible order, are not only the authors of language and of music, of
> the dance, and architecture, and statuary, and painting ; they
> are the institutors of laws and the founders of civil society, and
> the inventors of the arts of life, and the teachers who draw into
> a certain propinquity with the beautiful and the true that
> partial apprehension of the agencies of the invisible world

which is called religion......Poets, according to the circumstances of the age and nation in which they appeared, were called, in the earlier epochs of the world, legislators or prophets: a poet essentially comprises and unites both these characters. For he not only beholds intensely the present as it is, and discovers those laws according to which present things ought to be ordered, but he beholds the future in the present, and his thoughts are the germs of the flower and the fruit of latest time.

The last sentence in the above passage is an exact description of Shelley's own work as poet. And for this reason those readers who would understand the full significance of his poetry—even in such technical matters as rhythm and rhyme—must also understand the great ideas by which all his poetry is inspired. To assert that a sympathy with Shelley the pioneer is an obstacle to a right appreciation of Shelley the poet, is the crown of critical foolishness.

If we seek for a terse and comprehensive title for Shelley's poetical contribution to the literature and thought of his age, we shall call it the Poetry of Love. It is not merely that he was animated and heartened by this spirit of love. His language everywhere *speaks* love; and it is this that gives his style that distinctive tone of passionate tenderness which his predecessors had never imagined, and his followers have never been able to repeat. The correspondence between language and character was perfect in Shelley, and it was inevitable that both should be misapprehended by contemporary readers. "I know not the internal constitution of other men," he wrote in his essay *On Love*. "I see that in some external attributes they resemble me; but when, misled by that appearance, I have thought to appeal to something in common, and unburthen my inmost soul to them, I have found my language misunderstood, like one in a distant and savage land." And elsewhere: "Even in modern times no living poet ever arrived at the fullness of his fame; the jury which sits in judgment upon a poet, belonging as he does to all time, must be composed of his peers; it must be impannelled by Time from the selectest of the wise of many generations."

As we have seen, this posthumous recognition of Shelley's greatness as a poet has gone on apace; and his influence on succeeding literature, though he did not, like Wordsworth, leave a direct school of followers, has indirectly been very great. His triumph over the banded tyranny of critics has been unmistakable and complete, and above all other writers he has shown how absolutely the true singer can transcend what Macaulay termed "the irrational laws which bad critics have framed for the government of poets." So exemplary an overthrow of an all-powerful dogmatism could not fail to have important results; and it is no exaggeration to say that all later English poetry is largely indebted to Shelley for greater spirituality of thought, richer melody of tone, and fuller freedom of utterance. In an age of literary decadence, *his* star at least has suffered no obscurity or eclipse.

The fervid revolutionary era in which Shelley lived brought with it a corresponding enthusiasm of song. In Shelley's own words:—

The most unfailing herald, companion, and follower of the awakening of a great people to work a beneficial change in opinion or institution, is poetry. At such periods there is an accumulation of the power of communicating and receiving intense and impassioned conceptions respecting man and nature.......It is impossible to read the compositions of the most celebrated writers of the present day without being startled by the electric life which burns within their words.

By the year 1825, or thereabouts, this "electric life,"

which was most conspicuously manifested in the poetry
of Wordsworth, Shelley, and Byron, had spent its strength
and brilliancy. The vanguard of social and political
idealists, who in the early years of the century were
traversing a mountain-height of sanguine speculation,
and thence eagerly scanning the remoter vistas of the
future, had now to descend into an intervening valley of
temporary failure and disappointment, a humbler but not
less necessary period of toilsome effort and reconstruction.
In such a period there could be no great poetical outburst,
as in the time of the Revolution.

For the past ninety years English poetry has thus
been thrown back, as it were, on itself, and has been
busied rather in perfecting and polishing the standard
set by the great masters of 1775–1825 than in originating
any new conception of its own. The age of Tennyson
stands to the age of Burns and Wordsworth and Shelley
as did that of Theocritus to the great singers of Greece;
it is an aftermath, of rich fulfilment, indeed, and of
consummate technical art, but devoid of the energising
vitality of a new spirit. Take, for example, the relation
of Swinburne to Shelley. It is sometimes the fashion to
speak of " Shelley's mantle" as having descended on
Swinburne, or even to eulogise the later poet for having
carried to a still greater excellence the work which
Shelley had begun; and as far as metrical *technique* and
exuberance of language are concerned, the truth of the
comparison is obvious. But where, in Swinburne's
rhapsodies, however fluent and melodious, is a trace
of the *cor cordium*—that divine spirit of Love, which
broods like a benediction over Shelley's unrivalled lyrics,
and renders them, alike for melody and meaning, the
supreme achievement of modern English song?

CHAPTER X.

THE PIONEER

IN claiming for Shelley the title of pioneer, it is necessary to show that his deliberately adopted principles have in very fact anticipated and influenced the opinions of succeeding generations, and that, so far from being a purblind visionary who occasionally stumbled on a truth, he was a genuine and clear-eyed prophet of religious and political freedom.

The enormous progress made by freethought during the years that have passed since Shelley's death would in itself be sufficient refutation, if any were needed, of the assertion that he wrecked his judgment and good fame by his deliberate adoption of " atheistic " principles. He was from first to last an " atheist " in the sense that he denied the existence of the personal deity of the theologians ; though it is important to note that, as he himself says in the preface to *Laon and Cythna*, the object of his attack was " the erroneous and degrading idea which men have conceived of a Supreme Being, but not the Supreme Being itself "—it was not the presence, but the absence, of spirituality in the established creed that made Shelley an unbeliever.

I regard Shelley's early " atheism " and later " pantheism " as simply the negative and the affirmative sides of the same progressive but harmonious life-creed.   In his earlier years his disposition was towards a vehement denial of a theology which he never ceased to detest ; in his maturer years he made more frequent reference to

110

the great World-Spirit in whom he had from the first believed. He grew wiser in the exercise of his religious faith, but the faith was the same throughout; there was progression, but no essential change.

For holding and publishing these views he was ostracised and insulted; and now the same views are held as a matter of course by a vast number, probably a majority, of earnest and thoughtful men, the only difference being that the colourless title "agnosticism" has been substituted for the more expressive word which Shelley, with characteristic ardour, "took up and wore as a gauntlet."

It is the habit of Shelley's apologetic admirers to minimise the fact of his departure from the orthodox faith, and to suggest that, had he lived longer, he might, by some unexplained process of reasoning, have found himself at one with Christianity[1]—perhaps, according to Nathaniel Hawthorne's ironical suggestion, to the extent of taking holy orders and being "inducted to a small country living in the gift of the lord chancellor." Frederick Robertson's remark that Shelley knew nothing of Christianity but as "a system of exclusion and bitterness" was far from correct. It may be that Shelley had not carefully studied the historical development of Christianity; but the Bible was one of the books that were most often in his hands, and his knowledge of it might have put to shame many of those "religious" persons who regarded him as a scoffing "infidel." But the most important point of all to notice, in the consideration of this question, is that Shelley drew a strong line of

[1] It is entertaining to find the same apology made for Shakespeare, who, according to the *Times* (April 30, 1912), "was still in the experimental stage of life when he died," so that "it is not a reproach to him that he was not a great religious poet." Well, if Shakespeare also is among the novices, Shelley is in good company,

distinction between the character of Christ and the character of Christian; so that those who claim him as a possible convert to Christianity are laying stress on what tells against their own theory, when they point out his affinity to the spirit of Christ.

His own views on this subject may be seen in various passages of his writings, especially in the *Letter to Lord Ellenborough*, the *Essay on Christianity*, and the *Notes to Hellas*. In the last-mentioned work, written in the full maturity of his powers, he thus states his opinion of the contrast between Christ and Christian :—

> The sublime human character of Jesus Christ was deformed by an imputed identification with a power who tempted, betrayed, and punished the innocent beings who were called into existence by his sole will; and for the period of a thousand years the spirit of this most just, wise, and benevolent of men has been propitiated with myriads of hecatombs of those who approached the nearest to his innocence and wisdom, sacrificed under every aggravation of atrocity and variety of torture.

When we are told that Shelley, holding these views, would have ultimately embraced the Christian religion because of his sympathy with its founder, we can only reply that such an argument (to quote Shelley's own words) "presupposes that he who rejects Christianity must be utterly divested of reason and feeling."

It may be said that the gospel preached by Shelley was, like that of Christianity, a gospel of love. But here again the distinction between the teaching of Christ and the teaching of his followers is a vital one. And it must be noted that the love which Shelley inculcates is represented by him as resulting from the innate goodness, the natural benevolence of mankind, and not from any sense of religious obligation. Freethought and liberty are the

very basis of the Shelleyan morality, it being Shelley's
contention that virtue results from the intuitive desire to
promote the happiness of others, and that morality must
languish in proportion as freedom of thought and action
is withdrawn. This code of morals can scarcely be held
to be compatible with the doctrines of Christianity. If
Shelley had been merely sceptical, if his character had in
the slightest degree resembled that of Byron, there would
have been some colour for the notion that he would not
have always remained a recusant; but so far was he
from being simply an "honest doubter," on the look-out
for a religious creed, that he must be regarded as an
enthusiast of the strongest type, with a mission to
perform and a message to deliver.

It is generally recognised that two of the most
momentous social problems which press for solution are
the condition of the working classes and the emancipation of women; and it is a proof of the shrewdness of
Shelley's instinct that he, alone among the poets of his
era, strongly emphasised these two questions, anticipa-
ting in his conclusions the general principles, if not the
particular methods, of the policy to which modern
reformers incline.

It is true that, like Godwin, and indeed like all contemporary thinkers, with the possible exception of Robert
Owen, he was unable to grasp the full significance, in
its bearing on social questions, of the great industrial
development which the introduction of machinery brought
about: we cannot expect from Shelley an accurate knowledge of an economic change which in his time could
be only very imperfectly understood. But that he had a
singularly clear perception of the cardinal fact by which
the relations of labour and capital are characterised—the
fact that the poor workers support the lazy rich, and that

industry is taxed for the maintenance of idleness—is
obvious from many passages in his writings.

Here, for example, is a reference to the land question,
which states the case with admirable incisiveness and
vigour : " English reformers exclaim against sinecures,
but the true pension-list is the rent-roll of the landed
proprietors." And, again, of the extortions of the fund-
holders, those *nouveaux riches* whose heartless vulgarity
Shelley more than once condemns :—

> I put the thing in its simplest and most intelligible shape.
> The labourer, he that tills the ground and manufactures cloth,
> is the man who has to provide, out of what he would bring
> home to his wife and children, for the luxuries and comforts
> of those whose claims are represented by an annuity of forty-
> four millions a year levied upon the English nation.

Nor, while thus pointing out the actual dependence
of the so-called independent classes, did he evade the
consideration that he too, the scion of a wealthy house,
was a debtor in like manner ; he "shuddered to think"
that the roof which covered him and the bed on which
he slept were provided from the same source.

We see, therefore, that Shelley was well aware that
pauperism is no sporadic, unaccountable phenomenon,
but the necessary and logical counterpart of wealth, and
that the footsteps of luxury are for ever dogged by the
grim nemesis of destitution. Never perhaps has this
terrible truth been more powerfully stated than in the
description of the court masque in *Charles the First :*—

> Aye, there they are—
> Nobles, and sons of nobles, patentees,
> Monopolists, and stewards of this poor farm,
> On whose lean sheep sit the prophetic crows,
> Here is the pomp that strips the houseless orphan,
> Here is the pride that breaks the desolate heart.
> These are the lilies glorious as Solomon,

Who toil not, neither do they spin—unless
It be the webs they catch poor rogues withal.
Here is the surfeit which to them who earn
The niggard wages of the earth, scarce leaves
The tithe that will support them till they crawl
Back to her cold hard bosom. Here is health
Followed by grim disease, glory by shame,
Waste by lame famine, wealth by squalid want,
And England's sin by England's punishment.

An interesting saying of Karl Marx's—true of Shelley, though, I think, unjust to Byron—has been recorded in this connection. " The real difference between Byron and Shelley is this : Those who understand them and love them rejoice that Byron died at thirty-six, because if he had lived he would have become a reactionary bourgeois ; they grieve that Shelley died at twenty-nine, because he was essentially a revolutionist, and he would always have been one of the advanced guard of socialism." [1]

Shelley's views on the sex question are too well known to need more than a brief reference ; it is sufficient to point out that they are practically identical with those now held by the body of advanced thinkers. There is plenty of evidence in *Laon and Cythna* that he recognised and deplored the social subjection of woman, and the evil consequences that result therefrom to the other sex and to humanity in general. " Can man be free," he asks, " if woman be a slave ?"   And again :—

[1] "Shelley and Socialism," by Edward and Eleanor Marx Aveling. *To-Day*, April, 1888. The following is an extract from a letter written in 1892 by Karl Marx's daughter with reference to what she calls "the enormous influence of Shelley on one of the greatest and most practical movements of our time, the Chartist Movement": " I have heard my father and Engels again and again speak of this, and I have heard the same from the many Chartists it has been my good fortune to know as a child and young girl—Ernest Jones, Richard Moore, the Watsons, G. J. Harvey, and others. Engels said, ' Oh, we all knew Shelley by heart then.' Surely to have been one of the inspirers of such a movement is not bad for an ineffectual angel ! "

> Woman !—She is his slave, she has become
> A thing I weep to speak—the child of scorn,
> The outcast of a desolated home.
> Falsehood and fear and toil, like waves, have worn
> Channels upon her cheek, which smiles adorn,
> As calm decks the false ocean ; well ye know
> What Woman is, for none of Woman born
> Can choose but drain the bitter dregs of woe,
> Which ever from the oppressed to the oppressor flow.

The compulsion of the marriage-bond is explicitly condemned in the well-known *Notes to Queen Mab*, on the ground that, as the very essence of love is freedom of choice, society is not justified in imposing this restriction on the individual. That Shelley's views remained unchanged to the end may be gathered from the kindred, but maturer, passage of *Epipsychidion* :—

> I never was attached to that great sect
> Whose doctrine is that each one should select
> Out of the crowd a mistress or a friend,
> And all the rest, though fair and wise, commend
> To cold oblivion—though 'tis in the code
> Of modern morals, and the beaten road
> Which those poor slaves with weary footsteps tread
> Who travel to their home among the dead
> By the broad highway of the world—and so
> With one chained friend, perhaps a jealous foe,
> The dreariest and the longest journey go.

As it is, the Shelleyan advocacy of free love has been much misrepresented, being often absurdly identified, whether through ignorance or prejudice, with a heartless libertinism to which it is utterly alien. The essence of Shelley's belief was that, unless human passion is to be brutalised and debased, the spiritual and higher elements of love must always be present; for this reason he condemned the stereotyped and loveless formula of marriage, but he did not stultify his own contention by sanctioning an equally dull and loveless sensuality.

On this point it is worth while to note what he says in a short prose essay, written soon after *Queen Mab*, the review of his friend Hogg's novel, *Prince Alexy Haimatoff*. "The author," says Shelley, "appears to deem the loveless intercourse of brutal appetite a venial offence against delicacy and virtue! He asserts that a transient connection with a cultivated female may contribute to form the heart without essentially vitiating the sensibilities. It is our duty to protest against so pernicious and disgusting an opinion. No man can rise pure from the poisonous embraces of a prostitute, or sinless from the desolated hopes of a confiding heart."

Shelley's communism, like that of Godwin and other anarchist writers, was mingled with a very strong measure of individualism ; he believed that self-reform must precede, or at any rate accompany, all legislative enactments in those matters where, to quote his own expression, "every man possesses the power to legislate for himself." "Reform yourselves" is the chief lesson enforced in the *Address to the Irish People*, and in the *Essay on Christianity* the failure of the early Christian communism is attributed to the lack of a sufficient moral improvement.

The self-reform which he most persistently advocated may be summed up in the word *simplicity ;* his natural instincts were strong in the direction of the simple and the frugal; "genius joined to simplicity" was Byron's epitome of his character. Every reader of his life is aware how this tendency showed itself in his appearance, his dress, his diet ; he detested with his whole soul the exceeding discomfort of those so-called "comforts" of civilisation, which first impose a grievous burden on the drudges who produce them, and then turn out to be a curse, instead of a blessing, to those for whom they are produced. Here, in the appeal from a depraved habit to a natural liking, is the true "Return to Nature":—

> Our simple life wants little, and true taste
> Hires not the pale drudge Luxury, to waste
> The scene it would adorn, and therefore still,
> Nature, with all her children, haunts the hill.

The connection between simplicity and freedom, between naturalness and equality, is a most vital one, and no better exemplification of this union can be found than in the genius of Shelley. "All men," he says, "are called to participate in the community of Nature's gifts. The man who has fewest bodily wants approaches nearest to the Divine Nature. Satisfy these wants at the cheapest rate, and expend the remaining energies of your nature in the attainment of virtue and knowledge......In proportion as mankind becomes wise—yes, in exact proportion to that wisdom—should be the extinction of the unequal system under which they now subsist."

Liberty is in fact the final goal and outcome of simplicity; and such liberty—natural, equal, universal —is the very inspiration and keynote of Shelley's song. His ideal is the communist ideal of a society where free, spontaneous beneficence shall take the place of authority and government, where the reign of law shall be succeeded by the reign of love, where the simple kindly instincts of the human heart shall be holier than any code of religion or ethics.

Last but not least among these Shelleyan principles which may claim to have been confirmed and not negatived by time, are his humanitarian views, which include and underlie the rest. The crowning word both of his communism and individualism is Love, which is again and again inculcated in his writings as the one

supreme remedy for human suffering, the charm without
which all else is unavailing and unprofitable.

> To feel the peace of self-contentment's lot,
> To own all sympathies and outrage none,
> And in the inmost bowers of sense and thought,
> Until life's sunny day is quite gone down,
> To sit and smile with Joy, or, not alone,
> To kiss salt tears from the worn cheek of Woe;
> To live as if to love and live were one—
> This is not faith or law, nor those who bow
> To thrones on heaven or earth such destiny may know.

"To live as if to love and live were one"—that is a
true summary of Shelley's ethics. In accordance with
this spirit of unremitting gentleness, he deplored the
many acts of ferocious barbarism which disgraced, and
in great measure still disgrace, our boasted civilisation
—the savagery of modern warfare, the scarcely less
savage competition of commerce, the inhumanities of
our penal code, and the legalised murder known as
"capital punishment." He also followed Godwin in
deprecating all insurrectionary violence, and repeatedly
inveighed against the wickedness of revenge. "In recom-
mending a great and important change in the spirit
which animates the social institutions of mankind,"
thus he writes in the preface to *Laon and Cythna*, "I
have avoided all flattery to those violent and malignant
passions which are ever on the watch to mingle with
and to alloy the most beneficial innovations. There is no
quarter given to Revenge, or Envy, or Prejudice. Love
is celebrated everywhere as the sole law which should
govern the moral world."

Now, other poets have sung, before and after, of humanity and brotherhood; but there is just this peculiarity
about Shelley's method of handling these great themes.
He does not, as so many writers have done, eulogise

these virtues in the abstract, while shutting his eyes to
the many wrongs inflicted on "the lower classes," which,
albeit sanctioned by respectability and custom, render
real brotherhood impossible—on the contrary, he goes to
the heart of the matter, and denounces those evils which
are the most deadly sources of cruelty and oppression.
The true ruffian was to him (I quote his own words)
"the respectable man—the smooth, smiling, polished vil-
lain, whom all the city honours ; whose very trade is lies
and murder ; who buys his daily bread with the blood
and tears of men."

In similar manner, when touching on our relations
with "the lower animals," he did not, like a certain
school of sentimentalists, prate of men's benevolent feelings towards the objects of their gluttony, and preach
peace under conditions where peace does not exist ; but
boldly and consistently arraigned the prime cause of
animal suffering, the removal of which must precede the
establishment of a genuine human sympathy with the
lower races. Those who have knowledge of the recent
progress of vegetarianism are aware that here too, in his
condemnation of flesh-eating, Shelley was a precursor of
a vital and growing reform.

The importance of a man's dietetic tastes and habits
in their bearing on his character is too often overlooked
by critics and biographers. We hear much speculation
on the heredity of men of genius, and on the influence of
events contemporary with their birth and education ; but
the significance of the fact that the most ethereal of
English lyrists and one of the most unselfish of English
reformers was a bread-eater and a water-drinker is
allowed to pass unnoticed. Shelley's humanitarian
instincts and consequent inclination to extreme simplicity
of diet are regarded as a mere crotchet—and this, too, by

those very writers who praise his gospel of gentleness
and universal love! On this point some of Shelley's
detractors have done him more justice than his admirers;
for the former have at least been consistent in arguing
that his vegetarian proclivities were all of a piece with
his "pernicious" views on social and religious subjects,
and with his "utopian" belief in the ultimate perfectibility of man. We may surely assert that Shelley's
dietetic tastes must have had *some* influence on that
spirituality of tone which makes him unique among
singers.

In his practical politics Shelley was very far from being
swayed by that irreconcilable temper which is often supposed to be a mark of enthusiasts, for while always maintaining that "politics are only sound when conducted on
principles of morality," he was shrewd enough to see that
half a loaf is better than no bread. "Nothing is more
idle," he says in the *Philosophical View of Reform*, "than
to reject a limited benefit because we cannot without
great sacrifices obtain an unlimited one." "You know,"
he wrote to Leigh Hunt in 1819, "my principles incite
me to take all the good I can get in politics, for ever
aspiring to something more. I am one of those whom
nothing will fully satisfy, but who are ready to be
partially satisfied in all that is practicable."

That Shelley should, on some subjects, have been over-
cautious and moderate may seem surprising; yet it is a
fact that he pleaded for slowness and deliberation in cases
where the advanced radical opinion of to-day would
hardly be so long-suffering. He deprecated the abolition
of the crown and aristocracy until "the public mind,
through many gradations of improvement, shall have
arrived at the maturity which can disregard these sym-
bols of its childhood." He objected to the ballot as

being too mechanical a process of voting. He dis-approved of universal suffrage and of female suffrage as "somewhat immature," though he intimated that he was open to conviction on these points.

On national questions Shelley's sympathies were alto-gether with the party of freedom, and this not only when the struggle was located abroad (most poets and men of letters are enthusiastic over insurrections which are comfortably remote), but also when it was nearer home—let us say in Ireland—which is sometimes found to be a more searching test of a true passion for freedom. *Hellas*, the preface and notes of which are scarcely less remarkable for political insight than the poem itself for lyrical splendour, is a proof of Shelley's ardour in the Greek cause. "The wise and generous policy of Eng-land," he wrote, "would have consisted in establishing the independence of Greece, and in maintaining it both against Russia and the Turks; but when was the oppres-sor generous or just?"

The Dublin pamphlets, immature and almost boyish though they are in some respects, contain some wise fore-casts; and it is noticeable, as Mr. J. A. Symonds wrote, that "Catholic emancipation has, since Shelley's day, been brought about by the very measure he proposed and under the conditions he foresaw." The Union, again, was declared by Shelley to be a worse evil for Ireland than even the disqualification of Catholics; "the latter," he said, "affects few, the former affects thousands: the one disqualifies the rich from power, the other im-poverishes the peasant and adds beggary to the city."

Here, too, is Shelley's opinion on the subject of political "criminals": "Though the Parliament of England were to pass a thousand Bills to inflict upon those who deter-mined to utter their thoughts a thousand penalties, it could not render that criminal which was in its nature innocent before the passing of such a Bill." After more than a century of compulsory union and coercive legislation, the wisdom of this view is being slowly and painfully recognised by English politicians.

I have now mentioned certain of Shelley's revolutionary ideas which seem to be on the road to fulfilment, distant though the goal may still be ; and I have shown that, judged simply by the hard test of history and experience, such principles can no longer be contemptuously dismissed as visionary and unsubstantial. But what of those more prophetic yearnings and aspirations, those mystic glimpses into the equal and glorified humanity of the future, which, to those who can understand and sympathise with Shelley, are the very soul of his creed ? A learned and cultured critic has dogmatically asserted that Shelley's "abstract imagination set up arbitrary monstrosities of 'equality' and 'love,' which never will be realised among the children of men." But then, by the very nature of the case, it is not to the learned and cultured classes that Shelley's gospel will appeal, but rather to those whose conditions and surroundings have not incapacitated them for that most vital learning and only true culture—a belief in the brotherhood of mankind.

The ideal anarchism of which Shelley is the herald is a state of equality founded not on the competitive or baser element of human nature, but on the higher and ultimately more powerful element, which is love. "If there be no love among men," he says, "whatever institutions they may frame must be subservient to the same purpose—to the continuance of inequality. The only perfect and genuine republic is that which comprehends every living being." Nor is this beatified republic of Shelley's prophecy to be confined exclusively to the human race; it is all gentle and loving life, not human life only, that is the theme of his song :—

> No longer now the wingèd habitants,
> That in the woods their sweet lives sing away,
> Flee from the form of man ; but gather round,
> And prune their sunny feathers on the hands
> Which little children stretch in friendly sport
> Towards these dreadless partners of their play.
> All things are void of terror ; man has lost
> His terrible prerogative, and stands
> An equal amidst equals.

The fact that this distant vision of a golden age, of man " equal, unclassed, tribeless and nationless," takes little account of the intervening obstacles between the actual state and the ideal, is by no means a valid proof that the vision is a deceptive one. The traveller who discerns from afar the mountain-top which is the object of his pilgrimage cannot correctly calculate the many minor ridges which, though at the moment they make but little show in the landscape, must be laboriously and patiently surmounted before his ambition can be satisfied ; he knows that these difficulties are real, but he knows that the summit is real also.

It was inevitable that Godwin and Shelley, living before the age of evolutionary science, should under-estimate the vast scope and tenacity of hereditary forces in the moral as well as in the physical world, and should be over-sanguine as to the power of individual self-regeneration ; but it is an absurd error to suppose that Shelley expected a sudden miraculous change in the nature of man—a sort of cosmic transformation scene. It is true that in *Laon and Cythna* and *Prometheus Unbound* he used, as he was quite entitled to use, the license of a poet by concentrating into brief compass a revolution which must have demanded a long period for its accomplishment, little suspecting that his critics would attribute to him the almost incredible folly of a literal belief in the sudden extirpation of evil—a misconception which is the more astonishing because his utterances on this point are sufficiently numerous and conclusive.

In the Preface to *Laon and Cythna* itself he notes as one of the errors of the French Revolution which should henceforth be avoided, an expectation of " such a degree of unmingled good as it was impossible to realise." " Can he," says Shelley, " who the day before was a trampled slave, suddenly become liberal-minded, forbearing, and independent?......But mankind appear to be emerging from their trance. I am aware, methinks, of a slow, gradual, silent change. In that belief I have composed the following poem." And, again, in the Irish pamphlet : " We can expect little amendment in our own time, and we must be content to lay the foundation of liberty and happiness by virtue and wisdom." And yet again, in the *Philosophical View of Reform :* " It is no matter how slow, gradual, and cautious be the change."

There are one or two other prevalent misunderstandings of the Shelleyan ideals which could never have existed if his prose works had been read with any sort of attention, and if critics had taken ordinary trouble to distinguish Shelley the lyric poet and mythmaker from Shelley the philosopher and essayist. It has been assumed on the strength of passages in *Queen Mab* and elsewhere that he believed literally in a past golden age, from which Man, the one outcast of Nature, had miserably fallen. But though Shelley, writing as a poet, and with the just freedom of a poet, as in the great nature-myth of the *Prometheus Unbound*, speaks of a past Golden Age from which man has fallen, it is mere

misrepresentation to accuse him of a literal belief in any
such state of primeval happiness. So far from being
shattered by the theory of evolution, the Shelleyan
creed, as far as it goes, is distinctly in accordance
therewith, as may be seen from the following passage
of his *Essay on Christianity* :—

> The wisest and most sublime of the ancient poets......repre-
> sented equality as the reign of Saturn, and taught that mankind
> had gradually degenerated from the virtue which enabled
> them to enjoy or maintain this happy state. Their doctrine
> was philosophically false......Man was once as a wild beast ; he
> has become a moralist, a metaphysician, a poet, and an astro-
> nomer.

In his advocacy of natural habits, therefore, it is
evident that Shelley was not thinking of a relapse from
civilisation to barbarism—that bugbear which, strange to
say, is found anywhere rather than in the writings of those
who are supposed to be the authors of it. What he *did*
mean can fortunately be placed equally beyond dispute
by the quotation of his own words :—

> Nothing is more obviously false than that the remedy
> for the inequality among men consists in their return to the
> condition of savages and beasts.......Rousseau certainly did
> not mean to persuade the immense population of his country to
> abandon all the arts of life, destroy their habitations and their
> temples, and become the inhabitants of the woods. He
> addressed the most enlightened of his compatriots, and
> endeavoured to persuade them to set the example of a pure
> and simple life, by placing in the strongest point of view his
> conceptions of the calamitous and diseased aspect which, over-
> grown as it is with the vices of sensuality and selfishness, is
> exhibited by civilised society.[1]

The problem is further expressed by Shelley with
admirable clearness in the following sentence: " The
whole of human science is comprised in one question :

---

[1] *Essay on Christianity.*

How can the advantages of intellect and civilisation be reconciled with the liberty and pure pleasures of natural life ? How can we take the benefits, and reject the evils, of the system which is now interwoven with all the fibres of our being ? " [1]

Again, as regards the external origin of evil, we must guard against a too literal interpretation of passages which are by their very nature poetical. Shelley delights to personify the Manichæan doctrine of a good and an evil spirit, under the forms of the serpent and the eagle, of Prometheus and Jupiter ; but we shall do him gross injustice if we suppose him ignorant of the subtle mixture of the two elements in the human mind. He knew well that the sources of evil lie far back beyond the reach of scientific discovery ; indeed, he has himself remarked on " that intertexture of good and evil with which Nature seems to have clothed every form of individual existence." But he believed that the good was more essential and organic, and in that sense more "natural" than the evil, and that, in spite of temporary defeat, it was destined to be in the end victorious. Thus, in his personification of these rival powers, it is the liberty of Nature which is typified on the one hand, on the other the tyranny of Custom. This primal innocence, vitiated, but not extirpated, by the corruption of society, is the leading topic of *Queen Mab* :—

> Ah, to the stranger-soul, when first it peeps
> From its new tenement, and looks abroad
> For happiness and sympathy, how stern
> And desolate a tract is this wide world !
> How withered all the buds of natural good !
> No shade, no shelter from the sweeping storms
> Of pitiless power ! On its wretched frame,

[1] *Vindication of Natural Diet.*

Poisoned, perchance, by the disease and woe
Heaped on the wretched parent whence it sprung
By morals, law, and custom, the pure winds
Of Heaven, that renovate the insect tribes,
May breathe not. The untainting light of day
May visit not íts longings. It is bound
Ere it has life ; yea, all the chains are forged
Long ere its being : all liberty and love
And peace is torn from its defencelessness ;
Cursed from its birth, even from its cradle doomed
To abjectness and bondage !

It has been urged that Shelley's blissful view of wild
nature is altogether too rose-coloured, and in conflict
with the stern Darwinian discoveries of an internecine
warfare ; and it has been the fashion of late years to
quote Tennyson's description of " Nature red in tooth
and claw " as truer and more " scientific " than Shelley's.
But what say the modern naturalists ? " The poet's
picture of nature red in tooth and claw," says Dr. Alfred
R. Wallace, " is a picture the evil of which is read into it
by our imaginations, the reality being made up of full and
happy lives, usually terminated by the quickest and least
painful of deaths." [1] And Darwin himself remarks that,
" When we reflect on this struggle, we may console ourselves with the full belief that the war of nature is not
incessant, that no fear is felt, that death is generally
prompt, and that the vigorous and the happy survive
and multiply." It seems, then, that Shelley was fully
justified in contrasting the calm, instinctive happiness of
Nature, a happiness which is tried, but not destroyed, by
the struggle for existence, with the restless, self-conscious,
introspective miseries of Man. He did not, of course,
overlook the obvious fact—as obvious before Darwin as
after—that there is a competition in nature as well as in
human society.

[1] *Darwinism*, ch. ii.

Still less is it the case that he regarded kings and
priests as the originators of human wretchedness, however much he might charge them with fostering and
perpetuating it. "Government," he distinctly says, "is
in fact the mere badge of men's depravity. They are so
little aware of the inestimable benefits of mutual love as
to indulge, without thought, and almost without motive,
in the worst excesses of selfishness and malice. Hence,
without graduating human society into a scale of empire
and subjection, its very existence has become impossible."[1]
That Shelley had a hearty hatred of priestcraft and king-
ship, as types of intellectual and temporal despotism, is
beyond doubt; but he was not moved against them by
any such unreasoning antipathy as that with which he
is often credited.

The truth is that, so far from being, as his apologists
have represented him, at once the advocate and the
victim of certain benevolent but illusory ideas, which
fall to pieces the moment they are brought into contact
with the facts of science, Shelley was well in accord with
the most advanced knowledge of his age. The doctrine
of Perfectibility is an assertion not of a future sudden
perfection, but of the unlimited progressive tendency of
mankind, and as such is distinctly a scientific doctrine.
It has been truly said[2] that "by instinct, intuition,
whatever we have to call that fine faculty that feels
truths before they are put into definite shape, Shelley
was an evolutionist."

We have now seen what were in fact Shelley's principles and ideals, as contrasted with the imaginary
absurdities which critics have invented for him, to the

---

[1] *Essay on Christianity.*
[2] "Shelley and Socialism," by Edward and Eleanor Marx Aveling, *To-day*,
April, 1888.

utter distortion of his views and to their own exceeding
bewilderment; we have seen also how marked has been
the progress made by these ideas since the time when a
contemporary reviewer pronounced *Prometheus Unbound*
—the poem which we now begin to recognise as the great
modern epic of humanity—to be the "stupid trash of a
delirious dreamer," and accounted for the severity of this
judgment by remarking that it was "for the advantage of
sterling productions to discourage counterfeits."

Shelley was heart and soul a free-thinker; and freethought is now in the ascendant wherever men think at
all. He was an advocate of free love; and the failure of
marriage has become so notorious as to be a common-
place of modern novel-writers. He was a pioneer of
communism; and the vast spread of socialist doctrines is
the every-day complaint of a capitalist press. He was a
humanitarian; and humanitarianism, having survived
the phase of ridicule and misrepresentation, is taking
its place among the chief motive-powers of civilised
society.

Of Shelley's personal character I have already spoken,
and only this much need now be said, that the increasing
influence which it has exercised on successive generations
of readers tells its own tale. If certain critics cannot
understand the peculiar charm which others have felt
só keenly, a charm which for some of us has sweetened
life and strengthened all our hopes for mankind, they
will perhaps do wisely not to proclaim their own de-
ficiencies by declaring Shelley to be unintelligible. To the
sympathetic reader Shelley's moral nature is as little an
enigma as his writings; to the unsympathetic it is very
enigmatical indeed; but it does not follow that Shelley is
the party to be commiserated on that account—there is
an alternative which the hostile critic should introspec-

tively ponder before pronouncing adverse judgment on the accused poet.

Once more let me disclaim any idea of suggesting that Shelley was a faultless being (to mention one obvious reason to the contrary, he was unfortunate enough to be brought up in affluence and saved the necessity of earning his own living), or that it is desirable that anybody should pay him homage. I do but point out that his character is a typical one—typical of certain revolutionary ideals, by the rightness or wrongness of which it will ultimately stand or fall.

For all which reasons, is it not time that we finally divested ourselves of the notion of that weak, amiable, unscientific Shelley; that brilliant but eccentric visionary, with an exalted enthusiasm, a genius for lyric poetry, and a foolish aversion to priests and kings? The view each generation takes of a revolutionary writer is inevitably formed and coloured in great measure by the ethical and religious convictions prevalent for the time being. By the old-fashioned, uncompromising, brutal Toryism of a century back, a poet like Shelley could hardly have been regarded otherwise than as the foe of all that is respectable, the "fiend-writer" to whom contemporary critics ascribed a super-human malignity.

To the milder-mannered but somewhat inconsistent and invertebrate Liberalism of the succeeding period he became a grotesque mixture of good and evil qualities, no longer a demon downright, but a semi-celestial nondescript, " a beautiful and ineffectual angel, beating in the void his luminous wings in vain."

By the full-fledged social democracy on whose threshold we now stand, he will at length be seen in his true human character as the inspired prophet of a larger and saner morality, which will bring with it the realisation of the equality and freedom to which his whole life was so faithfully and ungrudgingly devoted.

And as for the years, or maybe the centuries, that must still elapse before the world shall see the fulfilment of those remoter Shelleyan ideals—of that splendid vision of the ultimate regeneration of mankind—does it behove us to be despondent? Must we not rather say of them, in the words of Prometheus himself :—

Perchance no thought can count them, yet they pass.

INDEX